MASTERING PYTHON FOR DATA ENGINEERING

Transform and Manipulate Big Data with Python

THOMPSON CARTER

TABLE OF CONTENTS

Introduction

Mastering Data Engineering: Building Robust Data Pipelines

Data engineering has become one of the most critical disciplines in the modern data-driven world. With the exponential growth of data across industries, the ability to manage, process, and analyze that data efficiently has become paramount. As businesses rely more heavily on data to drive decision-making, the role of data engineers is expanding to ensure that data is accessible, clean, and ready for analysis at scale. This book, *Mastering Data Engineering: Building Robust Data Pipelines*, is designed to provide both beginners and experienced professionals with a comprehensive understanding of data engineering concepts and the practical skills needed to build powerful data pipelines.

Why Data Engineering?

Data engineering plays a foundational role in the broader data ecosystem. While data scientists focus on deriving insights from data and building predictive models, data engineers are responsible for creating the infrastructure that allows data to flow seamlessly between systems, ensuring it is reliable, consistent, and accessible.

Whether it's batch processing for historical data, real-time data streaming, or implementing large-scale data lakes, data engineers are essential to transforming raw data into valuable business intelligence.

What This Book Offers

This book provides a hands-on, practical guide to building data engineering pipelines. It covers the entire process of building robust data pipelines, starting from the initial stages of data ingestion, followed by data cleaning and transformation, to ensuring data is stored efficiently and made accessible for analysis. Each chapter will introduce key tools, technologies, and frameworks used in data engineering, with real-world examples that help solidify understanding.

You'll learn how to work with databases, distributed systems, and cloud environments to build scalable, high-performance systems. We will dive deep into technologies like Apache Spark, Apache Kafka, Dask, and cloud-native platforms like AWS and GCP. In addition, we'll cover the critical aspects of workflow orchestration, real-time processing, and best practices for maintaining data pipelines.

What You'll Learn

- **Building Scalable Data Pipelines**: Learn how to design, implement, and scale data pipelines that can handle large volumes of data, both in real-time and in batch.

- **Data Processing Frameworks**: Master frameworks such as Apache Spark and Dask for distributed data processing and parallel computing to handle big data efficiently.

- **Data Ingestion and Storage**: Understand how to collect and store data from various sources using cloud technologies and tools like Amazon S3, Kafka, and NoSQL databases.

- **Workflow Orchestration**: Learn how to automate and manage complex data workflows using tools like Apache Airflow and Prefect, ensuring that your data pipeline operates smoothly.

- **Data Integration with BI Tools**: Explore how to integrate your data pipelines with popular business intelligence tools like Tableau and Power BI for visualization and reporting.

- **Best Practices for Data Governance**: Understand the importance of maintaining data quality, security, and compliance with data privacy regulations like GDPR and CCPA.

The Structure of This Book

This book is divided into 26 chapters, each focusing on a key aspect of data engineering. We begin with the basics—defining data engineering, understanding core concepts, and setting up your environment. From there, we cover the tools and technologies that enable building robust data pipelines, such as database management, distributed systems, cloud computing, and real-time processing.

Each chapter builds on the last, moving from basic concepts to more advanced topics. Real-world examples and use cases from industries like e-commerce, finance, and healthcare demonstrate how these concepts are applied in practice. By the end of the book, you will have the knowledge and practical experience to design and implement end-to-end data engineering workflows, from ingesting raw data to serving it for analysis and visualization.

***

Why This Book is for You

Whether you're a beginner in the data engineering field, an aspiring data engineer looking to deepen your knowledge, or an experienced professional seeking to stay updated on the latest tools and techniques, *Mastering Data Engineering* provides the insights and skills you need to succeed. The book is written in a jargon-free, accessible manner, ensuring that complex topics are explained in a way that anyone can understand.

This book is also designed for professionals who are eager to expand their toolkit with modern technologies. It emphasizes practical implementation, with real-world examples, step-by-step tutorials, and best practices that you can apply immediately in your projects. It also provides insights into the future of data engineering, preparing you for the evolving landscape of big data, cloud technologies, machine learning, and AI integration.

How to Use This Book

Each chapter in this book stands alone, so you can read through it sequentially or dive into specific areas of interest as needed. The chapters are structured to provide both conceptual explanations and hands-on examples, with exercises to reinforce what you've learned. You'll find practical code snippets and clear explanations that will help you build and optimize your own data engineering pipelines.

For beginners, the first few chapters will lay a solid foundation of data engineering concepts, tools, and techniques. For more experienced professionals, the later chapters provide advanced topics, such as cloud-native data pipelines, real-time streaming, and machine learning integrations, which will challenge you and offer fresh perspectives.

Data engineering is a dynamic and essential field that enables the modern data-driven world. By mastering the concepts, tools, and techniques presented in this book, you will be well-equipped to tackle the challenges of building scalable, efficient, and reliable data pipelines. The insights and skills you gain from this book will empower you to not only contribute to data engineering projects but also advance your career in this rapidly growing field.

Let's embark on this journey to master the art of data engineering and unlock the power of data pipelines that can drive meaningful insights and innovations.

Chapter 1: Introduction to Data Engineering

---

1. What is Data Engineering?

Data engineering is the backbone of modern data-driven organizations. It involves the design, construction, and maintenance of data pipelines that ensure the efficient collection, storage, transformation, and accessibility of data.

Key Responsibilities of Data Engineers:

1. **Data Collection**: Integrating data from various sources like databases, APIs, and files.
2. **Data Transformation**: Cleaning, normalizing, and structuring data to meet analytical needs.
3. **Data Storage**: Designing scalable and efficient data storage solutions, such as data warehouses and lakes.
4. **Data Delivery**: Ensuring data is accessible to analysts, data scientists, and applications.
5. **Data Governance**: Implementing measures to ensure data security, privacy, and compliance.

Why Data Engineering Matters:

- Organizations generate massive amounts of data daily.

- Clean, accessible data is essential for making informed decisions.
- Data engineers ensure data pipelines are reliable, scalable, and optimized.

Real-World **Example**:
An e-commerce platform relies on data engineering to collect customer behavior data, transform it into actionable insights, and deliver it to marketing teams for targeted campaigns.

---

2. Role of Python in Data Engineering

Python has become a cornerstone of data engineering due to its versatility, readability, and vast ecosystem of libraries and frameworks. It enables engineers to handle every stage of the data pipeline, from ingestion to analysis.

Why Python is Ideal for Data Engineering:

1. **Simplicity and Readability**: Python's clean syntax makes it easy to learn and implement.
2. **Extensive Libraries**: Libraries like pandas, SQLAlchemy, and PySpark simplify complex tasks.
3. **Integration Capabilities**: Python integrates seamlessly with databases, APIs, and big data frameworks.

4. **Community Support**: A vast community provides tools, tutorials, and troubleshooting help.

Key Python Libraries for Data Engineering:

- **Data Manipulation**: pandas, numpy
- **Data Storage**: SQLAlchemy, psycopg2, pymongo
- **Big Data**: PySpark, Dask
- **Workflow Automation**: airflow, prefect, luigi

Python   **in**   **Action**: A Python script using pandas can clean and aggregate customer purchase data before loading it into a database:

python

```
import pandas as pd

# Load data
data = pd.read_csv("sales_data.csv")

# Clean and aggregate
data['Total'] = data['Quantity'] * data['Price']
summary = data.groupby('Category')['Total'].sum()

# Save to a new file
summary.to_csv("category_summary.csv")
```

3. Overview of Tools and Frameworks for Data Engineering

Modern data engineering involves working with a wide range of tools and frameworks tailored for different stages of the data pipeline. Here's a high-level overview:

---

1. Data Ingestion Tools:

- **Apache Kafka**: Real-time data streaming platform.
- **Flume**: Efficiently collects, aggregates, and moves log data.
- **Python Libraries**: requests for APIs, BeautifulSoup for web scraping.

Example: Using requests to fetch data from an API:

python

```python
import requests

response = requests.get("https://api.example.com/data")
if response.status_code == 200:
    data = response.json()
```

---

2. Data Storage Solutions:

- **Relational Databases**: PostgreSQL, MySQL
- **NoSQL Databases**: MongoDB, Cassandra

- **Data Lakes**: AWS S3, Azure Blob Storage
- **Data Warehouses**: Snowflake, Google BigQuery, Amazon Redshift

Example: Using SQLAlchemy to interact with a PostgreSQL database:

python

```
from sqlalchemy import create_engine

engine = create_engine('postgresql://user:password@localhost/dbname')
data = pd.read_sql("SELECT * FROM sales", engine)
```

3. Data Processing Frameworks:

- **Apache Spark**: Distributed computing for large-scale data processing.
- **Dask**: Parallel computing in Python.
- **ETL Tools**: Airflow, Luigi, Prefect

Example: Using PySpark for distributed data processing:

python

```
from pyspark.sql import SparkSession

spark = SparkSession.builder.appName("DataProcessing").getOrCreate()
data = spark.read.csv("large_dataset.csv", header=True, inferSchema=True)
data.show()
```

4. Data Visualization and Reporting:

- **Visualization Tools**: Matplotlib, Seaborn, Plotly
- **Dashboarding Tools**: Tableau, Power BI, Dash, Shiny

Example: Visualizing data with Matplotlib:

python

```
import matplotlib.pyplot as plt

categories = ['Electronics', 'Clothing', 'Furniture']
sales = [25000, 15000, 10000]

plt.bar(categories, sales)
plt.title("Category-wise Sales")
plt.show()
```

5. Workflow Orchestration Tools:

- **Apache Airflow**: Schedule and monitor workflows.
- **Prefect**: Simplified orchestration with Pythonic syntax.
- **Luigi**: Build complex pipelines with task dependencies.

Example: Defining a task in Airflow:

python

```python
from airflow import DAG
from airflow.operators.python_operator import PythonOperator
from datetime import datetime

def my_task():
    print("Task executed!")

dag = DAG('example_dag', start_date=datetime(2023, 1, 1),
schedule_interval='@daily')
task = PythonOperator(task_id='my_task', python_callable=my_task, dag=dag)
```

Data engineering forms the foundation of data-driven organizations, ensuring the availability of clean, reliable, and actionable data. Python's simplicity, versatility, and extensive ecosystem make it an indispensable tool for building efficient data pipelines. As we proceed through this book, we'll delve deeper into the concepts, tools, and techniques that empower data engineers to transform raw data into meaningful insights, unlocking the full potential of data in today's world.

Chapter 2: Setting Up Your Python Environment

1. Installing Python and Essential Libraries

Before diving into data engineering, it's crucial to set up a robust Python environment. This ensures you have the tools and libraries needed to work efficiently with data.

1.1. Installing Python

Python can be downloaded and installed from the official Python website or using package managers like brew (MacOS) or apt (Linux).

- **Download and Install Python**:
  1. Visit python.org.
  2. Download the latest stable version.
  3. During installation:
     - Check the box to **Add Python to PATH**.
     - Enable optional features like pip.
- **Verify Installation**: After installation, open a terminal or command prompt and run:

  bash

```
python --version
```

or

```
bash
```

```
python3 --version
```

1.2. Installing Essential Libraries

Python libraries simplify common tasks in data engineering. Use pip, Python's package manager, to install them.

- **Install pip** (if not already installed):

```
bash
```

```
python -m ensurepip --upgrade
```

- **Install Libraries**:

```
bash
```

```
pip install pandas numpy matplotlib seaborn sqlalchemy psycopg2
pymongo requests
```

- **Key Libraries for Data Engineering**:
  - **pandas**: Data manipulation and analysis.
  - **numpy**: Numerical computations.
  - **sqlalchemy**: Database interactions.

- ○ **pymongo**: MongoDB connections.

- ○ **requests**: Accessing APIs.

- ○ **matplotlib and seaborn**: Data visualization.

2. Setting Up IDEs

Integrated Development Environments (IDEs) make coding more efficient with features like debugging, syntax highlighting, and integrated terminals. Below are some popular IDEs for Python development:

2.1. PyCharm

PyCharm is a feature-rich IDE specifically designed for Python development.

- **Installing PyCharm**:
    1. Visit jetbrains.com/pycharm.
    2. Download the Community Edition (free) or Professional Edition (paid).
- **Setting Up a Project in PyCharm**:
    1. Open PyCharm and create a new project.
    2. Set the interpreter to your Python installation under **File > Settings > Project: <project_name> > Python Interpreter**.

2.2. Visual Studio Code (VSCode)

VSCode is a lightweight, highly customizable editor with robust Python support.

- **Installing VSCode**:
  1. Download from code.visualstudio.com.
  2. Install the Python extension:
     - Open VSCode.
     - Go to **Extensions** (Ctrl+Shift+X or Cmd+Shift+X).
     - Search for "Python" and install it.
- **Setting Up a Python Project**:
  1. Open your project folder in VSCode.
  2. Set the interpreter:
     - Open the Command Palette (Ctrl+Shift+P or Cmd+Shift+P).
     - Search for **Python: Select Interpreter** and choose the installed Python version.

2.3. Jupyter Notebook

Jupyter Notebook provides an interactive environment ideal for exploratory data analysis and prototyping.

- **Installing Jupyter Notebook**: Install Jupyter with pip:

bash

pip install notebook

- **Launching Jupyter Notebook**:

bash

jupyter notebook

This opens a web-based interface where you can create and edit .ipynb files.

- **Key Features**:
  - Write and execute Python code in cells.
  - Combine code, markdown, and visualizations.
  - Export reports in multiple formats.

3. Introduction to Virtual Environments

Virtual environments isolate Python projects, ensuring dependencies do not conflict across projects.

3.1. Using venv

The venv module is included in Python's standard library and helps create isolated environments.

- **Create a Virtual Environment**:

bash

```
python -m venv myenv
```

This creates a directory myenv containing the isolated Python environment.

- **Activate the Virtual Environment**:
  - On Windows:

  bash

  ```
  myenv\Scripts\activate
  ```

  - On MacOS/Linux:

  bash

  ```
  source myenv/bin/activate
  ```

- **Install Libraries in the Virtual Environment**:

bash

```
pip install pandas numpy
```

- **Deactivate the Virtual Environment**:

  bash

  deactivate

3.2. Using conda

Conda is a powerful package manager and environment manager, particularly useful for data science.

- **Install Conda**: Download and install Anaconda or Miniconda from anaconda.com.
- **Create a Conda Environment**:

  bash

  conda create --name myenv python=3.9

- **Activate the Conda Environment**:

  bash

  conda activate myenv

- **Install Libraries**:

  bash

conda install pandas numpy

- **Deactivate the Conda Environment**:

bash

conda deactivate

- **Managing Environments**: List all environments:

bash

conda env list

---

4. Best Practices for Managing Python Environments

1. **Use Virtual Environments**: Always create a virtual environment for each project.
2. **Keep Dependencies Updated**: Regularly update libraries to avoid security and compatibility issues.
3. **Document Requirements**: Use pip freeze to save dependencies to a requirements.txt file.

bash

pip freeze > requirements.txt

Install dependencies from the file:

bash

```
pip install -r requirements.txt
```

4. **Use Version Control**: Track code changes using Git for better collaboration and rollback capabilities.

A well-configured Python environment is the foundation of effective data engineering. By setting up Python, essential libraries, and IDEs, and using virtual environments, you ensure a streamlined, conflict-free workflow. With your environment ready, you're equipped to dive into the world of data engineering and tackle real-world challenges efficiently. In the next chapter, we'll explore Python fundamentals tailored for data engineering.

Chapter 3: Python Fundamentals for Data Engineering

---

1. Variables, Data Types, and Basic Operations

Data engineering workflows rely on effectively manipulating and managing data. Python provides flexible and intuitive tools to work with various data types and operations.

1.1. Variables and Assignment

Variables store data values, which can be of different types.

- **Defining Variables**:

    python

    ```
    name = "Alice"  # String
    age = 30        # Integer
    salary = 75000.50  # Float
    is_manager = True  # Boolean
    ```

- **Dynamic Typing**: Python does not require explicit declaration of variable types. The type is inferred at runtime.
- **Type Checking**:

python

```
print(type(name))  # Output: <class 'str'>
```

1.2. Data Types

Python has several built-in data types that are essential for data engineering tasks.

- **Numeric Types**: int, float, complex

python

```
x = 10  # int
y = 5.5  # float
z = 3 + 4j  # complex
```

- **String**:

python

```
message = "Welcome to Data Engineering"
print(message.upper())     # Output: "WELCOME TO DATA ENGINEERING"
```

- **Boolean**:

python

```
is_valid = True
```

```python
print(not is_valid)  # Output: False
```

- **Collections**:
    - **List**:

    python

    ```python
    data = [1, 2, 3, 4]
    data.append(5)
    print(data)  # Output: [1, 2, 3, 4, 5]
    ```

    - **Dictionary**:

    python

    ```python
    record = {"name": "Alice", "age": 30}
    print(record["name"])  # Output: Alice
    ```

1.3. Basic Operations

- **Arithmetic Operations**:

python

```python
result = (10 + 5) * 3 / 2
print(result)  # Output: 22.5
```

- **String Operations**:

python

```python
fullname = "John" + " " + "Doe"
print(fullname)  # Output: John Doe
```

- **List Operations**:

python

```python
numbers = [1, 2, 3]
doubled = [n * 2 for n in numbers]
print(doubled)  # Output: [2, 4, 6]
```

2. Control Structures, Loops, and Functions

Control structures and loops allow you to create dynamic workflows, while functions encapsulate reusable logic.

2.1. Control Structures

- **Conditional Statements**:

python

```python
age = 18
if age >= 18:
    print("Adult")
else:
    print("Minor")
```

- **Nested Conditions**:

python

```python
score = 85
if score >= 90:
    print("Grade: A")
elif score >= 75:
    print("Grade: B")
else:
    print("Grade: C")
```

2.2. Loops

- **For Loop**:

python

```python
for i in range(5):
    print(i)  # Output: 0 1 2 3 4
```

- **While Loop**:

python

```python
n = 5
while n > 0:
    print(n)
    n -= 1  # Decrement n
```

- **Iterating Over Collections**:

python

```python
fruits = ["apple", "banana", "cherry"]
for fruit in fruits:
    print(fruit)
```

2.3. Functions

Functions make code reusable and modular, which is crucial in data engineering.

- **Defining a Function**:

python

```python
def greet(name):
    return f"Hello, {name}!"
print(greet("Alice"))  # Output: Hello, Alice!
```

- **Default Parameters**:

python

```python
def greet(name="Guest"):
    return f"Hello, {name}!"
print(greet())  # Output: Hello, Guest!
```

- **Lambda Functions**: Lambda functions are anonymous, single-expression functions.

  python

  ```
  square = lambda x: x ** 2
  print(square(4))  # Output: 16
  ```

3. Object-Oriented Programming Basics

Object-Oriented Programming (OOP) organizes code into reusable and maintainable classes and objects.

3.1. Classes and Objects

- **Defining a Class**:

  python

  ```
  class Employee:
      def __init__(self, name, age, position):
          self.name = name
          self.age = age
          self.position = position

      def display_info(self):
          return f"{self.name}, {self.age}, {self.position}"
  ```

```
# Creating an Object
emp1 = Employee("Alice", 30, "Data Engineer")
print(emp1.display_info())  # Output: Alice, 30, Data Engineer
```

3.2. Inheritance

Inheritance allows a class to inherit properties and methods from another class.

- **Example**:

  python

```
class Manager(Employee):
    def __init__(self, name, age, position, team_size):
        super().__init__(name, age, position)
        self.team_size = team_size

    def display_info(self):
        return f"{self.name}, {self.position}, Team Size: {self.team_size}"

manager = Manager("Bob", 40, "Team Lead", 5)
print(manager.display_info())  # Output: Bob, Team Lead, Team Size: 5
```

3.3. Encapsulation

Encapsulation restricts access to certain properties or methods to ensure data security.

- **Example**:

python

```
class Account:
    def __init__(self, balance):
        self.__balance = balance  # Private attribute

    def get_balance(self):
        return self.__balance

acc = Account(1000)
print(acc.get_balance())  # Output: 1000
```

Mastering Python fundamentals is essential for data engineering. Variables, data types, control structures, loops, and functions form the foundation for writing efficient scripts. Understanding object-oriented programming provides a modular approach to building scalable and maintainable solutions. Equipped with these skills, you're ready to manipulate data and design pipelines effectively. In the next chapter, we'll explore Python's advanced data structures and their applications in data engineering workflows.

Chapter 4: Working with Data Structures

1. Lists, Dictionaries, Sets, and Tuples

Data structures are foundational to Python programming and play a critical role in data engineering workflows. Selecting the right data structure impacts the performance, efficiency, and readability of your code.

1.1. Lists

Lists are ordered, mutable collections of items.

- **Creating and Manipulating Lists**:

  python

  ```python
  numbers = [10, 20, 30, 40]
  numbers.append(50)  # Add an item
  numbers.remove(20)  # Remove an item
  print(numbers)  # Output: [10, 30, 40, 50]
  ```

- **Common List Operations**:

  python

  ```python
  print(len(numbers))  # Output: 4
  ```

```python
print(numbers[0])  # Output: 10
print(numbers[-1])  # Output: 50
```

- **List Comprehensions**:

python

```python
squares = [x ** 2 for x in range(5)]
print(squares)  # Output: [0, 1, 4, 9, 16]
```

1.2. Dictionaries

Dictionaries store key-value pairs, offering fast lookups.

- **Creating and Accessing Dictionaries**:

python

```python
record = {"name": "Alice", "age": 30, "role": "Data Engineer"}
print(record["name"])  # Output: Alice
```

- **Adding and Removing Keys**:

python

```python
record["salary"] = 80000  # Add key-value pair
del record["role"]  # Remove a key
```

- **Iterating Through a Dictionary**:

python

```
for key, value in record.items():
    print(f"{key}: {value}")
```

1.3. Sets

Sets are unordered collections of unique elements.

- **Creating and Modifying Sets**:

python

```
fruits = {"apple", "banana", "cherry"}
fruits.add("orange")
fruits.discard("banana")
print(fruits)  # Output: {'orange', 'apple', 'cherry'}
```

- **Set Operations**:

python

```
set1 = {1, 2, 3}
set2 = {3, 4, 5}
print(set1.union(set2))  # Output: {1, 2, 3, 4, 5}
print(set1.intersection(set2))  # Output: {3}
```

1.4. Tuples

Tuples are immutable, ordered collections of items.

- **Creating and Accessing Tuples**:

  python

  dimensions = (1920, 1080)
  print(dimensions[0]) # Output: 1920

- **Why Use Tuples?**
  - Faster than lists for read-only operations.
  - Useful for fixed collections, like coordinates or settings.

---

2. Advanced Operations with collections Module

The collections module provides specialized data structures that extend Python's built-in types.

2.1. deque

A deque (double-ended queue) allows fast appends and pops from both ends.

- **Using deque**:

  python

```
from collections import deque

queue = deque(["Alice", "Bob", "Charlie"])
queue.append("Diana")
queue.popleft()  # Removes "Alice"
print(queue)  # Output: deque(['Bob', 'Charlie', 'Diana'])
```

2.2. defaultdict

A defaultdict provides default values for missing keys.

- **Using defaultdict**:

python

```
from collections import defaultdict

counts = defaultdict(int)
words = ["apple", "banana", "apple"]
for word in words:
    counts[word] += 1
print(counts)  # Output: defaultdict(<class 'int'>, {'apple': 2, 'banana': 1})
```

2.3. Counter

A Counter counts occurrences of elements in an iterable.

- **Using Counter**:

python

```
from collections import Counter

data = ["apple", "banana", "apple", "cherry"]
counts = Counter(data)
print(counts)  # Output: Counter({'apple': 2, 'banana': 1, 'cherry': 1})
```

2.4. OrderedDict

An OrderedDict preserves the insertion order of items.

- **Using OrderedDict**:

python

```
from collections import OrderedDict

ordered = OrderedDict()
ordered["a"] = 1
ordered["b"] = 2
ordered["c"] = 3
print(ordered)  # Output: OrderedDict([('a', 1), ('b', 2), ('c', 3)])
```

3. Data Structure Selection for Performance Optimization

Choosing the right data structure depends on the specific requirements of your workflow.

3.1. When to Use Each Data Structure

Data Structure	Use Case
List	Ordered collection with frequent inserts and lookups by index.
Dictionary	Fast lookups and modifications using keys.
Set	Ensuring uniqueness or performing set operations like union and intersection.
Tuple	Immutable collections, ideal for fixed data like coordinates.
deque	Fast appends and pops from both ends in a queue or stack.
defaultdict	Automatic handling of missing keys with default values.
Counter	Counting occurrences in a dataset.

3.2. Performance Considerations

- **Time Complexity**:

- ○ **List Lookup**: $O(n)O(n)O(n)$ (linear search).

- ○ **Dictionary Lookup**: $O(1)O(1)O(1)$ (hash-based).

- ○ **Set Operations**: $O(1)O(1)O(1)$ for add/remove.

- **Memory Usage**:

  - ○ Tuples use less memory compared to lists due to immutability.

  - ○ Avoid overusing defaultdict or Counter for large datasets where memory is critical.

- **Real-World Example**: Optimizing a word frequency counter:

python

```
from collections import Counter

with open("large_text.txt", "r") as file:
    text = file.read().split()
word_counts = Counter(text)
print(word_counts.most_common(5))  # Top 5 frequent words
```

Understanding Python's data structures is fundamental to writing efficient and readable code. Lists, dictionaries, sets, and tuples serve as the backbone for most data engineering tasks, while advanced tools from the collections module provide flexibility for specialized scenarios. Choosing the right data structure based on the task and optimizing for performance ensures scalable and maintainable solutions. In the next chapter, we'll dive into data ingestion and learn how to read, write, and transform data using Python.

Chapter 5: Introduction to Big Data Concepts

1. Understanding Big Data and Its Challenges

Big data refers to datasets that are too large, complex, or fast-changing to be handled efficiently by traditional data processing systems. These datasets require specialized tools, frameworks, and approaches to extract meaningful insights.

1.1. Characteristics of Big Data

Big data is defined by the "4Vs"—Volume, Velocity, Variety, and Veracity:

1. **Volume**: The sheer size of data generated from sources like social media, IoT devices, and transaction logs.

    o **Example**: Petabytes of data collected by e-commerce platforms to track user behavior.

2. **Velocity**: The speed at which data is generated, collected, and processed.

    o **Example**: Real-time stock market data updates.

3. **Variety**: The diversity of data formats, such as structured (databases), semi-structured (JSON, XML), and unstructured (images, videos, text).
    - o **Example**: A company processing customer feedback from emails, reviews, and support chats.
4. **Veracity**: The accuracy and reliability of data, often impacted by biases, errors, or incomplete information.
    - o **Example**: Cleaning and validating social media data with noise and misinformation.

1.2. Challenges of Big Data

1. **Storage**: Traditional relational databases may struggle to store and manage large datasets.
2. **Processing**: Handling the speed and complexity of big data requires distributed computing frameworks.
3. **Integration**: Combining data from various formats and sources into a unified system.
4. **Security and Privacy**: Protecting sensitive data while maintaining compliance with regulations like GDPR.

2. Key Concepts: Volume, Velocity, Variety, and Veracity
2.1. Volume

- Big data solutions often rely on scalable storage systems such as:
  - **HDFS (Hadoop Distributed File System)**: Splits data into chunks across multiple nodes.
  - **Cloud Storage**: Services like AWS S3, Azure Blob Storage.

2.2. Velocity

- Real-time processing systems are essential for high-velocity data.
  - **Examples**:
    - Apache Kafka for streaming data ingestion.
    - Apache Flink for real-time analytics.

2.3. Variety

- Data engineers must handle diverse data formats:
  - **Structured**: Tables in relational databases.
  - **Semi-structured**: JSON, XML, YAML.
  - **Unstructured**: Images, videos, audio files.

2.4. Veracity

- Data cleaning and validation tools, such as:
  - **OpenRefine** for manual data cleansing.
  - **Python Libraries**:

python

import pandas as pd

# Cleaning missing values
df = pd.read_csv("data.csv")
df.fillna("N/A", inplace=True)

3. Overview of Distributed Systems and Data Pipelines

Distributed systems allow data to be stored, processed, and analyzed across multiple machines, enabling scalability and fault tolerance.

3.1. What Are Distributed Systems?

A distributed system is a collection of interconnected machines working together as a single system.

- **Key Features**:
    - **Scalability**: Can handle growing datasets by adding more nodes.
    - **Fault Tolerance**: Ensures reliability even if some nodes fail.
    - **Parallel Processing**: Tasks are divided among multiple nodes for faster execution.
- **Examples**:

- o Apache Hadoop for distributed storage and batch processing.
- o Apache Spark for in-memory distributed computing.

3.2. Key Components of a Distributed System

1. **Storage Layer**:
   - o HDFS: Stores data in distributed chunks.
   - o Amazon S3: Scalable cloud storage for big data.
2. **Processing Layer**:
   - o Apache Spark: Handles large-scale data processing in memory.
   - o Apache Flink: Ideal for real-time data stream processing.
3. **Coordination Layer**:
   - o **Apache ZooKeeper**: Manages distributed applications and ensures synchronization.

3.3. What Are Data Pipelines?

A data pipeline is a sequence of steps that extract, transform, and load (ETL) data from one system to another.

- • **Steps in a Data Pipeline**:
  1. **Extract**:

- Pull data from sources like APIs, databases, or log files.

2. **Transform**:
   - Clean, aggregate, or enrich data for analysis.
3. **Load**:
   - Store data into a target system, such as a database or data warehouse.

- **Example Pipeline**:

1. Extract data from an API using Python's requests library.
2. Transform the data using pandas.
3. Load the processed data into a PostgreSQL database using SQLAlchemy.

3.4. Tools for Building Data Pipelines

1. **Apache Airflow**:
   - Workflow orchestration tool for scheduling and monitoring ETL jobs.

python

```
from airflow import DAG
from airflow.operators.python_operator import PythonOperator
from datetime import datetime
```

```
def extract_data():
    print("Data extracted")

dag = DAG('example_dag', start_date=datetime(2023, 1, 1),
schedule_interval='@daily')

task = PythonOperator(task_id='extract_task',
python_callable=extract_data, dag=dag)
```

2. **Apache NiFi**:
   - o Drag-and-drop interface for building data pipelines.
3. **Prefect**:
   - o Python-native workflow orchestration.
4. **Luigi**:
   - o Simplifies task dependencies in complex workflows.

3.5. Batch vs. Streaming Pipelines

1. **Batch Processing**:
   - o Processes data in chunks at scheduled intervals.
   - o Tools: Apache Hadoop, Spark Batch.
2. **Streaming Processing**:
   - o Processes data continuously as it arrives.
   - o Tools: Apache Kafka, Spark Streaming, Apache Flink.

4. Real-World Example: End-to-End Data Pipeline

Scenario: A retail company wants to analyze sales data from multiple stores in near real-time.

- **Pipeline Design**:
    1. **Extract**: Collect data from store databases using APIs.
    2. **Transform**: Aggregate sales by category and clean missing values.
    3. **Load**: Store the transformed data in a cloud-based data warehouse like Snowflake.

- **Implementation**:

python

```
import pandas as pd
import requests
from sqlalchemy import create_engine

# Step 1: Extract
response = requests.get("https://api.retail.com/sales")
raw_data = response.json()

# Step 2: Transform
df = pd.DataFrame(raw_data)
df['total_sales'] = df['quantity'] * df['price']
cleaned_data = df.dropna()
```

```
# Step 3: Load
engine = create_engine('postgresql://user:password@host:port/dbname')
cleaned_data.to_sql('sales', engine, if_exists='replace', index=False)
```

Understanding big data concepts and their associated challenges is critical for data engineers. The 4Vs—Volume, Velocity, Variety, and Veracity—illustrate the complexity of working with big data, while distributed systems and data pipelines provide the tools to handle these challenges effectively. In the next chapter, we'll explore how to ingest data from various sources, including files, APIs, and databases.

Chapter 6: Data Ingestion with Python

Data ingestion is the first step in building a data pipeline. It involves gathering data from various sources, transforming it into a usable format, and storing it for further analysis. This chapter explores how to use Python to read and write files, access databases, and extract data from APIs and websites.

1. Reading and Writing Files

Python offers built-in modules and libraries like csv, json, openpyxl, and pandas for working with different file formats.

1.1. CSV Files

CSV (Comma-Separated Values) files are one of the most commonly used formats for storing tabular data.

- **Reading CSV Files**:

    python

    import csv

    with open('data.csv', mode='r') as file:

```
reader = csv.reader(file)
for row in reader:
    print(row)
```

- **Writing CSV Files**:

python

```
with open('output.csv', mode='w', newline='') as file:
    writer = csv.writer(file)
    writer.writerow(['Name', 'Age', 'Role'])
    writer.writerow(['Alice', 30, 'Data Engineer'])
```

- **Using pandas for CSV**:

python

```
import pandas as pd

# Read CSV
df = pd.read_csv('data.csv')
print(df.head())

# Write CSV
df.to_csv('output.csv', index=False)
```

1.2. JSON Files

JSON (JavaScript Object Notation) is widely used for APIs and semi-structured data.

- **Reading JSON Files**:

python

```
import json

with open('data.json', mode='r') as file:
    data = json.load(file)
    print(data)
```

- **Writing JSON Files**:

python

```
data = {'name': 'Alice', 'age': 30, 'role': 'Data Engineer'}

with open('output.json', mode='w') as file:
    json.dump(data, file, indent=4)
```

1.3. Excel Files

Excel files are commonly used in business reporting.

- **Using openpyxl for Excel**:

python

```
from openpyxl import load_workbook

# Read Excel
```

```
workbook = load_workbook('data.xlsx')
sheet = workbook.active
for row in sheet.iter_rows(values_only=True):
    print(row)
```

- **Using pandas for Excel**:

python

```
# Read Excel
df = pd.read_excel('data.xlsx')
print(df.head())

# Write Excel
df.to_excel('output.xlsx', index=False)
```

2. Accessing Databases

Python provides several libraries to interact with relational and NoSQL databases.

2.1. Using SQLAlchemy

SQLAlchemy is a powerful ORM (Object-Relational Mapper) for interacting with databases.

- **Connecting to a Database**:

python

```
from sqlalchemy import create_engine

engine = create_engine('sqlite:///example.db')
connection = engine.connect()
```

- ## Executing Queries:

python

```
result = connection.execute("SELECT * FROM employees")
for row in result:
    print(row)
```

- ## Loading Data with pandas:

python

```
# Read from database
df = pd.read_sql("SELECT * FROM employees", connection)

# Write to database
df.to_sql('new_table', engine, if_exists='replace', index=False)
```

2.2. Using pymysql

pymysql is a lightweight library for connecting to MySQL databases.

- ## Connecting to MySQL:

```
python
```

```
import pymysql
```

```
connection = pymysql.connect(
    host='localhost',
    user='root',
    password='password',
    database='test_db'
)
```

```
cursor = connection.cursor()
```

- **Executing Queries**:

```
python
```

```
cursor.execute("SELECT * FROM employees")
for row in cursor.fetchall():
    print(row)
```

3. Consuming APIs

APIs (Application Programming Interfaces) allow applications to communicate and exchange data. Python's requests library makes it easy to consume APIs.

3.1. Using the requests Library

- **Making a GET Request**:

python

```python
import requests

response = requests.get("https://api.example.com/data")
if response.status_code == 200:
    data = response.json()
    print(data)
```

- **Making a POST Request**:

python

```python
payload = {'key': 'value'}
response = requests.post("https://api.example.com/data", json=payload)
print(response.json())
```

- **Handling Errors**:

python

```python
try:
    response = requests.get("https://api.example.com/data")
    response.raise_for_status()
except requests.exceptions.RequestException as e:
    print(f"Error: {e}")
```

4. Web Scraping for Data Extraction

When APIs are unavailable, web scraping can be used to extract data from websites. Python libraries like BeautifulSoup and scrapy are popular for this purpose.

4.1. Using BeautifulSoup

- **Scraping a Web Page**:

  python

  ```python
  from bs4 import BeautifulSoup
  import requests

  url = "https://example.com"
  response = requests.get(url)
  soup = BeautifulSoup(response.content, 'html.parser')

  # Extract data
  titles = soup.find_all('h2')
  for title in titles:
      print(title.text)
  ```

4.2. Using scrapy

scrapy is a framework for advanced web scraping.

- **Basic Scrapy Workflow**:

1. Install Scrapy:

   bash

   ```
   pip install scrapy
   ```

2. Start a project:

   bash

   ```
   scrapy startproject myproject
   ```

3. Define a spider in the spiders/ directory:

   python

   ```python
   import scrapy

   class ExampleSpider(scrapy.Spider):
       name = "example"
       start_urls = ["https://example.com"]

       def parse(self, response):
           for title in response.css('h2::text'):
               yield {"title": title.get()}
   ```

4. Run the spider:

   bash

   ```
   scrapy crawl example -o output.json
   ```

Data ingestion is a critical step in any data engineering workflow. Python provides powerful libraries to handle various data sources, including files, databases, APIs, and web pages. Mastering these tools allows data engineers to seamlessly extract, clean, and load data for downstream processing. In the next chapter, we'll focus on data cleaning and preprocessing techniques to prepare raw data for analysis.

Chapter 7: Data Cleaning and Preprocessing

Data cleaning and preprocessing are essential steps in preparing raw data for analysis. Clean and well-structured data ensures accurate results in downstream processes like data modeling and visualization. This chapter covers how to handle missing data, perform data type transformations, and address duplicates and outliers using Python.

1. Handling Missing Data

Missing data is common in real-world datasets and can significantly impact analysis if not handled properly. Python's pandas library provides robust tools for identifying and dealing with missing values.

1.1. Identifying Missing Data

- **Check for Missing Values**:

  python

  import pandas as pd

```
data = pd.DataFrame({
    'Name': ['Alice', 'Bob', None],
    'Age': [25, None, 30],
    'Salary': [50000, 60000, None]
})
print(data.isnull())  # Boolean mask of missing values
print(data.isnull().sum())  # Count of missing values per column
```

1.2. Handling Missing Values

- **Removing Missing Data**:
  - Drop rows with missing values:

    python

    ```
    cleaned_data = data.dropna()
    ```

  - Drop columns with missing values:

    python

    ```
    cleaned_data = data.dropna(axis=1)
    ```

- **Filling Missing Data**:
  - Fill with a constant:

    python

    ```
    data['Age'].fillna(0, inplace=True)
    ```

o Fill with statistical measures:

python

```python
data['Salary'].fillna(data['Salary'].mean(), inplace=True)
```

1.3. Advanced Techniques

- **Interpolate Missing Values**: Useful for time series data.

python

```python
data['Salary'] = data['Salary'].interpolate()
```

- **Imputation with Machine Learning**: Use predictive models to estimate missing values.

python

```python
from sklearn.impute import SimpleImputer

imputer = SimpleImputer(strategy='mean')
data['Age'] = imputer.fit_transform(data[['Age']])
```

2. Data Type Transformations

Ensuring the correct data types is crucial for accurate computations and operations. Mismatched data types can cause errors or inefficiencies.

2.1. Checking Data Types

- **Inspect Column Types**:

python

```
print(data.dtypes)
```

2.2. Converting Data Types

- **Convert to Numeric**: Convert a column to numeric, handling errors:

python

```
data['Age'] = pd.to_numeric(data['Age'], errors='coerce')
```

- **Convert to String**:

python

```
data['Name'] = data['Name'].astype(str)
```

- **Convert to Datetime**:

python

```
data['Date'] = pd.to_datetime(data['Date'])
```

2.3. Handling Categorical Data

- **Label Encoding**: Convert categories to numeric labels:

  python

  data['Category'] = data['Category'].astype('category').cat.codes

- **One-Hot Encoding**: Create binary columns for each category:

  python

  encoded_data = pd.get_dummies(data, columns=['Category'])

3. Dealing with Duplicates and Outliers

3.1. Identifying and Removing Duplicates

- **Find Duplicates**:

  python

  print(data.duplicated()) # Boolean mask of duplicates

- **Remove Duplicates**:

python

```
data = data.drop_duplicates()
```

3.2. Identifying Outliers

Outliers are extreme values that deviate significantly from the rest of the data. They can distort analysis and models.

- **Using Descriptive Statistics**:

python

```
print(data.describe())
```

- **Using Boxplots**: Visualize outliers with Matplotlib or Seaborn:

python

```
import matplotlib.pyplot as plt

plt.boxplot(data['Salary'].dropna())
plt.show()
```

- **Using the IQR (Interquartile Range)**:

python

```
Q1 = data['Salary'].quantile(0.25)
```

```
Q3 = data['Salary'].quantile(0.75)
IQR = Q3 - Q1


outliers = data[(data['Salary'] < Q1 - 1.5 * IQR) | (data['Salary'] > Q3 +
1.5 * IQR)]
print(outliers)
```

3.3. Handling Outliers

- **Remove Outliers**:

python

```
data = data[~((data['Salary'] < Q1 - 1.5 * IQR) | (data['Salary'] > Q3 +
1.5 * IQR))]
```

- **Transform Outliers**: Apply log transformation to reduce skewness:

python

```
data['Salary'] = data['Salary'].apply(lambda x: np.log(x) if x > 0 else x)
```

4. Practical Example: End-to-End Data Cleaning

Scenario: Clean a dataset with missing values, incorrect data types, duplicates, and outliers.

python

```python
import pandas as pd
import numpy as np

# Load data
data = pd.read_csv('raw_data.csv')

# Handle missing values
data['Age'].fillna(data['Age'].mean(), inplace=True)

# Convert data types
data['Date'] = pd.to_datetime(data['Date'])

# Remove duplicates
data = data.drop_duplicates()

# Handle outliers
Q1 = data['Salary'].quantile(0.25)
Q3 = data['Salary'].quantile(0.75)
IQR = Q3 - Q1
data = data[~((data['Salary'] < Q1 - 1.5 * IQR) | (data['Salary'] > Q3 + 1.5 * IQR))]

# Save cleaned data
data.to_csv('cleaned_data.csv', index=False)
```

Data cleaning and preprocessing are indispensable for ensuring the quality of your data and the accuracy of your analysis. Handling missing values, ensuring proper data types, and addressing duplicates and outliers are key steps in preparing raw data for further processing. In the next chapter, we'll explore how to manipulate and analyze data using Python's powerful pandas library.

Chapter 8: Data Manipulation with pandas

The **pandas** library is a cornerstone of Python's data analysis ecosystem. It provides high-performance, easy-to-use data structures like **DataFrames** and **Series**, enabling efficient manipulation and analysis of structured data. This chapter explores how to use pandas to filter, sort, group, merge, and join datasets effectively.

1. Introduction to pandas: DataFrames and Series

1.1. What is pandas?

pandas is a Python library designed for data manipulation and analysis. It introduces two key data structures:

- **Series**: One-dimensional array with labeled indices.
- **DataFrame**: Two-dimensional table with rows and columns, similar to a spreadsheet or SQL table.

1.2. Creating a Series

A **Series** is like a one-dimensional array with labels.

- **Create a Series**:

  python

  import pandas as pd

  data = pd.Series([10, 20, 30], index=['a', 'b', 'c'])
  print(data)
  Output:

  css

  a   10
  b   20
  c   30
  dtype: int64

- **Accessing Elements**:

  python

  print(data['b']) # Output: 20

1.3. Creating a DataFrame

A **DataFrame** is a two-dimensional structure with labeled rows and columns.

- **Create a DataFrame from a Dictionary**:

python

```python
data = pd.DataFrame({
    'Name': ['Alice', 'Bob', 'Charlie'],
    'Age': [25, 30, 35],
    'Salary': [50000, 60000, 70000]
})
print(data)
```

Output:

markdown

```
   Name  Age  Salary
0  Alice  25   50000
1   Bob  30   60000
2 Charlie 35  70000
```

- **Access Columns**:

python

```python
print(data['Name'])  # Output: Series of names
```

- **Access Rows**:

python

```python
print(data.iloc[1])  # Access by position
print(data.loc[0])   # Access by index
```

2. Filtering, Sorting, and Grouping Data

2.1. Filtering Data

- **Filter Rows by Condition**:

python

```
filtered_data = data[data['Age'] > 25]
print(filtered_data)
```

Output:

markdown

```
   Name  Age  Salary
1   Bob   30   60000
2 Charlie 35   70000
```

- **Filter Using Multiple Conditions**:

python

```
filtered_data = data[(data['Age'] > 25) & (data['Salary'] > 55000)]
```

2.2. Sorting Data

- **Sort by a Column**:

python

```
sorted_data = data.sort_values('Salary', ascending=False)
print(sorted_data)
```

- **Sort by Multiple Columns**:

python

```
sorted_data = data.sort_values(['Age', 'Salary'], ascending=[True, False])
```

2.3. Grouping Data

Grouping allows you to perform operations on subsets of data.

- **Group by a Column**:

python

```
grouped = data.groupby('Age')
print(grouped['Salary'].mean())  # Average salary by age
```

- **Apply Aggregate Functions**:

python

```
stats = data.groupby('Age').agg({
    'Salary': ['mean', 'sum'],
    'Name': 'count'
```

```
})
print(stats)
```

---

3. Merging and Joining Datasets

3.1. Concatenating DataFrames

Concatenate multiple DataFrames along rows or columns.

- **Concatenate Along Rows**:

python

```
df1 = pd.DataFrame({'Name': ['Alice'], 'Age': [25]})
df2 = pd.DataFrame({'Name': ['Bob'], 'Age': [30]})
result = pd.concat([df1, df2], ignore_index=True)
print(result)
```

Output:

markdown

```
    Name  Age
0  Alice   25
1    Bob   30
```

- **Concatenate Along Columns**:

python

```
result = pd.concat([df1, df2], axis=1)
```

3.2. Merging DataFrames

Merge two DataFrames based on a common column or index.

- **Inner Join**:

    python

    ```
    df1 = pd.DataFrame({'ID': [1, 2], 'Name': ['Alice', 'Bob']})
    df2 = pd.DataFrame({'ID': [1, 3], 'Salary': [50000, 60000]})
    result = pd.merge(df1, df2, on='ID', how='inner')
    print(result)
    ```

    Output:

    ```
      ID  Name  Salary
    0  1  Alice  50000
    ```

- **Left Join**:

    python

    ```
    result = pd.merge(df1, df2, on='ID', how='left')
    ```

- **Outer Join**:

    python

```
result = pd.merge(df1, df2, on='ID', how='outer')
```

3.3. Joining on Indices

If the index is meaningful, you can join DataFrames on their indices.

- **Join by Index:**

  python

  ```
  df1 = pd.DataFrame({'Salary': [50000, 60000]}, index=['Alice', 'Bob'])
  df2 = pd.DataFrame({'Age': [25, 30]}, index=['Alice', 'Bob'])
  result = df1.join(df2)
  print(result)
  ```
  Output:

  markdown

  ```
        Salary  Age
  Alice  50000   25
  Bob    60000   30
  ```

4. Practical Example: End-to-End Data Manipulation

Scenario: Prepare sales data for analysis by cleaning, aggregating, and merging datasets.

python

```
import pandas as pd
```

```python
# Load datasets
sales = pd.read_csv('sales.csv')
products = pd.read_csv('products.csv')

# Filter data for a specific region
sales = sales[sales['Region'] == 'North']

# Add a calculated column
sales['Total'] = sales['Quantity'] * sales['Price']

# Group sales by product ID
summary = sales.groupby('ProductID').agg({
    'Total': 'sum',
    'Quantity': 'sum'
}).reset_index()

# Merge with product details
final_data = pd.merge(summary, products, on='ProductID', how='left')

# Sort by total sales
final_data = final_data.sort_values('Total', ascending=False)

print(final_data.head())
```

The **pandas** library provides a powerful toolkit for data manipulation, offering capabilities to filter, sort, group, merge, and join datasets efficiently. Mastering these operations enables you to prepare and analyze data effectively, laying the foundation for advanced data engineering tasks. In the next chapter, we'll explore data visualization techniques to communicate insights visually.

Chapter 9: Data Visualization

Data visualization is a critical skill for data engineers and analysts to transform raw data into meaningful insights. By using libraries like **Matplotlib**, **Seaborn**, and **Plotly**, you can create static and interactive visualizations that effectively communicate your findings. This chapter will guide you through the fundamentals of visualizing data and crafting compelling visual stories.

1. Visualizing Data with Matplotlib and Seaborn

1.1. Introduction to Matplotlib

Matplotlib is a versatile library for creating static plots in Python. It provides control over every aspect of a plot, from layout to styling.

- **Basic Plot**:

    python

    import matplotlib pyplot as plt

    # Line plot
    x = [1, 2, 3, 4]
    y = [10, 20, 25, 30]

```python
plt.plot(x, y)
plt.title("Line Plot")
plt.xlabel("X-axis")
plt.ylabel("Y-axis")
plt.show()
```

- **Customizing Plots**:

  python

  ```python
  plt.plot(x, y, color='green', linestyle='--', marker='o')
  plt.grid(True)
  ```

- **Common Plot Types**:

  python

  ```python
  # Bar plot
  plt.bar(['A', 'B', 'C'], [10, 20, 15])
  plt.show()

  # Scatter plot
  plt.scatter(x, y)
  plt.show()
  ```

1.2. Introduction to Seaborn

Seaborn builds on Matplotlib, offering a high-level interface for creating attractive and informative statistical graphics.

- **Basic Plot**:

python

```python
import seaborn as sns
import pandas as pd

data = pd.DataFrame({
    'Category': ['A', 'B', 'C', 'D'],
    'Values': [10, 15, 13, 17]
})

sns.barplot(x='Category', y='Values', data=data)
```

- **Heatmaps**:

python

```python
import numpy as np

matrix = np.random.rand(5, 5)
sns.heatmap(matrix, annot=True, cmap='coolwarm')
```

- **Pair Plots**:

python

```python
sns.pairplot(data, diag_kind='kde')
```

2. Creating Interactive Dashboards with Plotly

2.1. Introduction to Plotly

Plotly is a powerful library for creating interactive visualizations. It supports a wide range of charts, including line charts, bar charts, scatter plots, and dashboards.

- **Basic Plot**:

    python

    ```python
    import plotly.express as px

    df = pd.DataFrame({
        'X': [1, 2, 3, 4],
        'Y': [10, 20, 25, 30]
    })

    fig = px.line(df, x='X', y='Y', title='Interactive Line Chart')
    fig.show()
    ```

- **Bar Chart**:

    python

    ```python
    fig = px.bar(df, x='X', y='Y', title='Interactive Bar Chart')
    fig.show()
    ```

2.2. Building Dashboards with Dash

Dash is a framework built on top of Plotly for creating interactive, web-based dashboards.

- **Basic Dash App**:

python

```python
from dash import Dash, dcc, html

app = Dash(__name__)

app.layout = html.Div([
    html.H1("Simple Dashboard"),
    dcc.Graph(
        figure=px.bar(df, x='X', y='Y', title='Bar Chart')
    )
])

if __name__ == '__main__':
    app.run_server(debug=True)
```

- **Adding Interactivity**:

python

```python
from dash import Input, Output

app.layout = html.Div([
    dcc.Dropdown(
        id='dropdown',
```

```
    options=[
        {'label': 'Line Chart', 'value': 'line'},
        {'label': 'Bar Chart', 'value': 'bar'}
    ],
    value='line'
),
dcc.Graph(id='graph')
])


@app.callback(
    Output('graph', 'figure'),
    Input('dropdown', 'value')
)
def update_chart(chart_type):
    if chart_type == 'line':
        return px.line(df, x='X', y='Y')
    else:
        return px.bar(df, x='X', y='Y')


if __name__ == '__main__':
    app.run_server(debug=True)
```

3. Visual Storytelling for Data Insights

Visual storytelling involves crafting a narrative using data visualizations to make insights more engaging and understandable.

3.1. Choosing the Right Chart Type

- **Line Chart**: Trends over time.
- **Bar Chart**: Comparisons between categories.
- **Scatter Plot**: Relationships between two variables.
- **Pie Chart**: Proportions in a dataset.
- **Heatmap**: Relationships in matrix data.

3.2. Annotating Charts

Adding annotations helps highlight key points.

- **Adding Text to Plots**:

  python

```
plt.plot(x, y)
plt.annotate('Key Point', xy=(2, 20), xytext=(3, 25),
        arrowprops=dict(facecolor='black', arrowstyle='->'))
plt.show()
```

3.3. Using Colors Effectively

Colors should emphasize important elements without overwhelming the viewer.

- **Seaborn Palette**:

  python

```python
sns.set_palette('coolwarm')
```

- **Custom Colors**:

python

```python
sns.barplot(x='Category', y='Values', data=data, color='skyblue')
```

3.4. Highlighting Insights

Focus on key takeaways:

- Use bold or larger font for critical labels.
- Add trendlines or markers for significant data points.

4. Practical Example: End-to-End Visualization

Scenario: Visualize and analyze sales data.

python

```python
import pandas as pd
import plotly.express as px

# Load data
data = pd.DataFrame({
    'Month': ['Jan', 'Feb', 'Mar', 'Apr'],
    'Sales': [1000, 1500, 2000, 2500],
    'Profit': [200, 300, 400, 500]
```

```
})

# Line Chart for Sales
fig1 = px.line(data, x='Month', y='Sales', title='Monthly Sales')
fig1.show()

# Bar Chart for Profit
fig2 = px.bar(data, x='Month', y='Profit', title='Monthly Profit')
fig2.show()

# Combined Dashboard
from dash import Dash, dcc, html

app = Dash(__name__)
app.layout = html.Div([
    html.H1("Sales Dashboard"),
    dcc.Graph(figure=fig1),
    dcc.Graph(figure=fig2)
])

if __name__ == '__main__':
    app.run_server(debug=True)
```

Data visualization is a powerful tool for understanding and communicating insights. With **Matplotlib** and **Seaborn**, you can create detailed static plots, while **Plotly** and **Dash** enable dynamic and interactive visualizations. By combining these tools with effective storytelling techniques, you can make your data more accessible and impactful. In the next chapter, we'll explore advanced visualization techniques and best practices for creating professional-grade dashboards.

Chapter 10: Data Pipelines and Workflow Automation

Data pipelines are essential for automating the movement, transformation, and storage of data, enabling organizations to maintain up-to-date and clean datasets for analysis. This chapter focuses on understanding ETL processes, building pipelines with Python, and scheduling tasks with tools like cron and Apache Airflow.

1. Understanding ETL (Extract, Transform, Load) Processes

1.1. What is ETL?

ETL stands for:

- **Extract**: Retrieve data from various sources (databases, APIs, files).
- **Transform**: Clean, normalize, and prepare data for analysis.
- **Load**: Store data in a target system like a data warehouse or database.

1.2. Components of ETL

1. **Extract**:
   - Sources: APIs, CSV files, databases, logs, etc.
   - Tools: Python libraries like requests, pandas, pymysql.

2. **Transform**:
   - Operations: Removing duplicates, handling missing values, aggregating data.
   - Tools: Libraries like pandas and numpy.

3. **Load**:
   - Destinations: Relational databases, NoSQL databases, or cloud storage.
   - Tools: Libraries like SQLAlchemy, psycopg2.

1.3. Benefits of ETL

- **Automation**: Reduces manual intervention.
- **Consistency**: Ensures data is clean and structured.
- **Scalability**: Handles large volumes of data efficiently.

---

2. *Building Pipelines with Python*

Python provides flexible libraries for building ETL pipelines. Below is an example of a simple pipeline using Python.

2.1. Step 1: Extract Data

Extract data from a CSV file and an API.

python

```
import pandas as pd
import requests

# Extract data from a CSV file
csv_data = pd.read_csv('sales_data.csv')

# Extract data from an API
response = requests.get('https://api.example.com/sales')
api_data = response.json()
```

2.2. Step 2: Transform Data

Clean and normalize the extracted data.

python

```
# Clean CSV data
csv_data.dropna(inplace=True)
csv_data['Total'] = csv_data['Quantity'] * csv_data['Price']

# Normalize API data
api_df = pd.DataFrame(api_data)
api_df['Date'] = pd.to_datetime(api_df['Date'])
```

2.3. Step 3: Load Data

Save the transformed data to a database.

python

```
from sqlalchemy import create_engine

engine = create_engine('sqlite:///sales.db')

# Save CSV data to the database
csv_data.to_sql('sales_csv', con=engine, if_exists='replace', index=False)

# Save API data to the database
api_df.to_sql('sales_api', con=engine, if_exists='replace', index=False)
```

2.4. Creating a Modular Pipeline

Build a reusable pipeline function.

python

```
def etl_pipeline(csv_file, api_url, db_url):
    # Extract
    csv_data = pd.read_csv(csv_file)
    response = requests.get(api_url)
    api_data = pd.DataFrame(response.json())

    # Transform
    csv_data.dropna(inplace=True)
```

```python
csv_data['Total'] = csv_data['Quantity'] * csv_data['Price']
api_data['Date'] = pd.to_datetime(api_data['Date'])

# Load
engine = create_engine(db_url)
csv_data.to_sql('sales_csv', con=engine, if_exists='replace', index=False)
api_data.to_sql('sales_api', con=engine, if_exists='replace', index=False)

# Run the pipeline
etl_pipeline('sales_data.csv', 'https://api.example.com/sales', 'sqlite:///sales.db')
```

3. Scheduling Tasks with cron and Airflow

Automating the execution of pipelines ensures timely updates of datasets.

3.1. Scheduling with cron

cron is a Unix-based tool for scheduling tasks.

- **Basic Syntax**:

  bash

  * * * * * command_to_run

  - o The five fields represent:
    - Minute (0-59)

- Hour (0-23)
- Day of the Month (1-31)
- Month (1-12)
- Day of the Week (0-7, 0 and 7 represent Sunday)

- **Schedule a Python Script**:

  - Open the crontab editor:

  bash

  crontab -e

  - Add an entry to run a script every day at 2 AM:

  bash

  0 2 * * * /usr/bin/python3 /path/to/etl_pipeline.py

  - Save and exit.

- **View Scheduled Tasks**:

bash

crontab -l

3.2. Scheduling with Apache Airflow

Apache Airflow is a robust platform for programmatically authoring, scheduling, and monitoring workflows.

- **Installing Airflow**:

  bash

  pip install apache-airflow

- **Setting Up Airflow**:
  1. Initialize the database:

     bash

     airflow db init

  2. Start the web server and scheduler:

     bash

     airflow webserver --port 8080
     airflow scheduler

- **Defining a DAG**: A Directed Acyclic Graph (DAG) defines a pipeline's tasks and dependencies.

  python

  from airflow import DAG
  from airflow.operators.python_operator import PythonOperator

```python
from datetime import datetime

def extract():
    print("Extracting data")

def transform():
    print("Transforming data")

def load():
    print("Loading data")

default_args = {
    'owner': 'airflow',
    'depends_on_past': False,
    'start_date': datetime(2023, 1, 1),
    'retries': 1
}

dag = DAG(
    'etl_pipeline',
    default_args=default_args,
    schedule_interval='@daily'
)

extract_task           =            PythonOperator(task_id='extract',
python_callable=extract, dag=dag)
transform_task         =            PythonOperator(task_id='transform',
python_callable=transform, dag=dag)
load_task = PythonOperator(task_id='load', python_callable=load,
dag=dag)
```

extract_task >> transform_task >> load_task

- **Monitoring the Pipeline**: Access the Airflow dashboard at http://localhost:8080 to monitor and manage the DAG.

---

4. Real-World Example: Automated Sales Data Pipeline

Scenario: Automate a daily pipeline to aggregate sales data from multiple sources and store it in a database.

1. **Pipeline Script**: Save the ETL logic in sales_etl.py.
2. **Schedule with Airflow**: Define an Airflow DAG to run sales_etl.py daily.

python

```python
from airflow import DAG
from airflow.operators.bash_operator import BashOperator
from datetime import datetime

default_args = {'owner': 'airflow', 'start_date': datetime(2023, 1, 1)}

dag    =    DAG('daily_sales_etl',    default_args=default_args,
schedule_interval='@daily')

etl_task = BashOperator(
    task_id='run_etl',
    bash_command='python3 /path/to/sales_etl.py',
```

```
    dag=dag
)
```

Data pipelines and workflow automation are critical for maintaining efficient and reliable data processes. By understanding ETL concepts, building pipelines with Python, and leveraging tools like cron and Apache Airflow, you can create scalable and automated workflows. In the next chapter, we'll explore relational databases and how to interact with them in Python.

Chapter 11: Working with Relational Databases

Relational databases are a cornerstone of data storage and management in data engineering. This chapter introduces SQL fundamentals, shows how to connect to relational databases using Python libraries like sqlite3 and psycopg2, and discusses query optimization techniques to enhance performance.

1. Introduction to SQL for Data Engineering

SQL (Structured Query Language) is used to interact with relational databases. It allows you to query, insert, update, and manage data efficiently.

1.1. Basic SQL Commands

- **Creating Tables**:

sql

```
CREATE TABLE employees (
    id SERIAL PRIMARY KEY,
    name VARCHAR(50),
```

```
age INT,
department VARCHAR(50),
salary FLOAT
);
```

- **Inserting Data**:

sql

```sql
INSERT INTO employees (name, age, department, salary)
VALUES ('Alice', 30, 'Engineering', 75000);
```

- **Querying Data**:

sql

```sql
SELECT * FROM employees;
```

- **Updating Data**:

sql

```sql
UPDATE employees
SET salary = 80000
WHERE name = 'Alice';
```

- **Deleting Data**:

sql

```sql
DELETE FROM employees
```

WHERE age < 25;

- **Filtering and Sorting**:

sql

```sql
SELECT name, salary
FROM employees
WHERE salary > 70000
ORDER BY salary DESC;
```

1.2. Advanced SQL Concepts

- **Joins**: Combine data from multiple tables:

sql

```sql
SELECT employees.name, departments.department_name
FROM employees
JOIN departments ON employees.department = departments.id;
```

- **Aggregation**: Perform calculations on groups of data:

sql

```sql
SELECT department, AVG(salary) AS avg_salary
FROM employees
GROUP BY department;
```

- **Indexes**: Speed up queries by indexing frequently queried columns:

  sql

  CREATE INDEX idx_salary ON employees(salary);

2. Connecting to Databases with Python

Python provides libraries like sqlite3 and psycopg2 to connect to relational databases. These libraries enable you to execute SQL commands and manage database interactions programmatically.

2.1. Connecting to SQLite with sqlite3

SQLite is a lightweight, serverless database engine ideal for small applications.

- **Creating and Connecting to a Database**:

  python

  import sqlite3

  ```
  # Connect to database (creates a new one if it doesn't exist)
  connection = sqlite3.connect("example.db")
  cursor = connection.cursor()
  ```

- **Executing SQL Queries**:

python

```
# Create a table
cursor.execute('''CREATE     TABLE     employees     (id     INTEGER
PRIMARY KEY, name TEXT, age INTEGER)''')

# Insert data
cursor.execute('''INSERT  INTO  employees  (name,  age)  VALUES
('Alice', 30)''')

# Commit changes
connection.commit()

# Query data
cursor.execute('''SELECT * FROM employees''')
rows = cursor.fetchall()
print(rows)
```

- **Closing the Connection**:

python

```
connection.close()
```

2.2. Connecting to PostgreSQL with psycopg2

PostgreSQL is a powerful, open-source relational database system suitable for large-scale applications.

- **Installing psycopg2**:

bash

pip install psycopg2

- **Connecting to PostgreSQL**:

python

```python
import psycopg2

connection = psycopg2.connect(
    dbname="testdb",
    user="postgres",
    password="password",
    host="localhost",
    port="5432"
)
cursor = connection.cursor()
```

- **Executing SQL Queries**:

python

```python
# Create a table
cursor.execute('''CREATE TABLE employees (id SERIAL PRIMARY KEY, name VARCHAR(50), age INT)''')

# Insert data
```

```
cursor.execute("'INSERT INTO employees (name, age) VALUES
('Bob', 25)'")

# Commit changes
connection.commit()

# Query data
cursor.execute("'SELECT * FROM employees'")
rows = cursor.fetchall()
print(rows)
```

- **Closing the Connection**:

```python
connection.close()
```

3. Query Optimization and Performance Tuning

Optimizing SQL queries ensures efficient execution and reduces system load.

3.1. Indexing

Indexes speed up data retrieval by creating a data structure that allows fast lookups.

- **Creating an Index**:

sql

```
CREATE INDEX idx_name ON employees(name);
```

- **When to Use Indexes**:
  - Columns frequently used in WHERE, JOIN, or ORDER BY clauses.
  - Avoid indexing columns with low cardinality (few unique values).

3.2. Avoiding Full Table Scans

Full table scans occur when the database reads every row in a table to execute a query.

- **Example**:

sql

```
SELECT * FROM employees WHERE salary > 70000;
```

Add an index on the salary column to improve performance:

sql

```
CREATE INDEX idx_salary ON employees(salary);
```

3.3. Query Execution Plans

Use EXPLAIN to understand how a query is executed and identify bottlenecks.

- **Example**:

  sql

  EXPLAIN SELECT * FROM employees WHERE salary > 70000;

3.4. Partitioning

Partitioning divides a large table into smaller, more manageable pieces.

- **Example**: Partition a table by range:

  sql

  CREATE TABLE employees_2023 PARTITION OF employees FOR VALUES FROM ('2023-01-01') TO ('2023-12-31');

3.5. Caching

Reduce redundant computations by caching query results.

- **Example**: Enable query caching in PostgreSQL using an extension like pgbouncer.

4. Practical Example: End-to-End Database Interaction

Scenario: Store and query sales data in PostgreSQL.

python

```python
import psycopg2
import pandas as pd

# Connect to PostgreSQL
connection = psycopg2.connect(
    dbname="salesdb",
    user="postgres",
    password="password",
    host="localhost",
    port="5432"
)
cursor = connection.cursor()

# Create a table
cursor.execute('''
CREATE TABLE IF NOT EXISTS sales (
    id SERIAL PRIMARY KEY,
    product VARCHAR(50),
    quantity INT,
    price FLOAT
)
''')

# Insert data
```

```
data = [('Laptop', 10, 1000.0), ('Phone', 20, 500.0)]
cursor.executemany("'INSERT INTO sales (product, quantity, price) VALUES
(%s, %s, %s)'", data)
connection.commit()

# Query data into a pandas DataFrame
query = "'SELECT product, quantity, price, quantity * price AS total FROM
sales'"
df = pd.read_sql(query, connection)
print(df)

# Close connection
connection.close()
```

Relational databases are essential for structured data storage and management. This chapter covered SQL fundamentals, how to interact with databases using Python, and techniques for optimizing queries. With these skills, you can efficiently handle large datasets and ensure high-performance database interactions. In the next chapter, we'll explore working with NoSQL databases and their use cases in modern data engineering.

Chapter 12: Working with NoSQL Databases

NoSQL databases have become a vital part of modern data engineering, enabling flexible and scalable data storage solutions for unstructured and semi-structured data. This chapter introduces NoSQL databases, demonstrates how to use MongoDB with pymongo, and explores querying and indexing techniques for optimizing NoSQL operations.

1. Introduction to NoSQL and Its Types

NoSQL databases are designed to handle diverse data models that traditional relational databases struggle to support. They are particularly effective for big data and real-time applications.

1.1. Characteristics of NoSQL Databases

- **Scalability**: Horizontal scaling to handle large volumes of data.
- **Flexibility**: Schema-less structure allows for dynamic changes to data models.
- **High Performance**: Optimized for specific types of queries and workloads.
- **Replication and Fault Tolerance**: Ensures data availability and reliability.

1.2. Types of NoSQL Databases

1. **Document-Oriented**:
   - o Stores data as documents (JSON-like structures).
   - o Example: MongoDB, CouchDB.
   - o Use Case: Content management systems, catalogs.

2. **Key-Value**:
   - o Stores data as key-value pairs.
   - o Example: Redis, DynamoDB.
   - o Use Case: Caching, session management.

3. **Column-Family**:
   - o Organizes data into columns instead of rows.
   - o Example: Apache Cassandra, HBase.
   - o Use Case: Time-series data, analytics.

4. **Graph**:
   - o Represents data as nodes and edges for relationships.
   - o Example: Neo4j, Amazon Neptune.
   - o Use Case: Social networks, fraud detection.

2. Using MongoDB with *pymongo*

MongoDB is one of the most popular NoSQL databases. It stores data in JSON-like documents and provides powerful querying capabilities.

2.1. Installing and Setting Up MongoDB

- **Install MongoDB**:
    - o Follow the installation guide for your OS at mongodb.com.
- **Start MongoDB**:

bash

mongod --dbpath /path/to/data

- **Install pymongo**:

bash

pip install pymongo

2.2. Connecting to MongoDB with pymongo

- **Connect to a MongoDB Database**:

python

from pymongo import MongoClient

client = MongoClient("mongodb://localhost:27017/")
db = client["mydatabase"] # Create or access a database

2.3. Inserting Documents

- **Insert a Single Document**:

python

```
collection = db["employees"]
employee = {"name": "Alice", "age": 30, "department": "Engineering"}
collection.insert_one(employee)
```

- **Insert Multiple Documents**:

python

```
employees = [
    {"name": "Bob", "age": 25, "department": "HR"},
    {"name": "Charlie", "age": 35, "department": "Finance"}
]
collection.insert_many(employees)
```

2.4. Querying Documents

- **Find All Documents**:

python

```
for doc in collection find():
    print(doc)
```

- **Find Documents with Filters**:

python

```
query = {"age": {"$gt": 30}}  # Find employees older than 30
for doc in collection.find(query):
    print(doc)
```

- **Find Specific Fields**:

python

```
projection = {"_id": 0, "name": 1, "department": 1}
for doc in collection.find({}, projection):
    print(doc)
```

2.5. Updating Documents

- **Update a Single Document**:

python

```
query = {"name": "Alice"}
new_values = {"$set": {"age": 31}}
collection.update_one(query, new_values)
```

- **Update Multiple Documents**:

python

```
query = {"department": "HR"}
new_values = {"$set": {"department": "Human Resources"}}
```

```
collection.update_many(query, new_values)
```

2.6. Deleting Documents

- **Delete a Single Document**:

python

```
collection.delete_one({"name": "Charlie"})
```

- **Delete Multiple Documents**:

python

```
collection.delete_many({"department": "Finance"})
```

3. *Querying and Indexing in NoSQL Databases*

Indexes play a critical role in optimizing queries in NoSQL databases.

3.1. Query Operators in MongoDB

- **Comparison Operators**:

python

```
query = {"age": {"$gte": 30}}  # Greater than or equal to 30
```

- **Logical Operators**:

python

```python
query = {"$and": [{"age": {"$gte": 30}}, {"department": "Engineering"}]}
```

- **Regex Search**:

python

```python
query = {"name": {"$regex": "^A"}}  # Names starting with 'A'
```

3.2. Indexing in MongoDB

Indexes improve the performance of read operations by reducing the amount of data scanned.

- **Create an Index**:

python

```python
collection.create_index("name") # Single-field index
```

- **Compound Index**:

python

```python
collection.create_index([("department", 1), ("age", -1)])  # 1 for ascending, -1 for descending
```

- **View Existing Indexes**:

python

```
print(collection.index_information())
```

- **Drop an Index**:

python

```
collection.drop_index("name_1")
```

3.3. Performance Considerations

- **Avoid Over-Indexing**: Too many indexes can slow down write operations.
- **Shard Data**: Distribute large datasets across multiple nodes for scalability.
- **Use Projections**: Return only necessary fields to reduce payload size.

4. Practical Example: Employee Management System

Scenario: Build a MongoDB-based system to manage employee records.

python

```python
from pymongo import MongoClient

# Connect to MongoDB
client = MongoClient("mongodb://localhost:27017/")
db = client["company"]

# Create a collection
employees = db["employees"]

# Insert employees
employees.insert_many([
    {"name": "Alice", "age": 30, "department": "Engineering"},
    {"name": "Bob", "age": 25, "department": "HR"},
    {"name": "Charlie", "age": 35, "department": "Finance"}
])

# Query employees in the Engineering department
query = {"department": "Engineering"}
projection = {"_id": 0, "name": 1, "age": 1}
for emp in employees.find(query, projection):
    print(emp)

# Update department name
employees.update_one({"department": "HR"}, {"$set": {"department": "Human Resources"}})

# Create an index on the name field
employees.create_index("name")

# View all employees
```

```
for emp in employees.find():
  print(emp)
```

NoSQL databases like MongoDB provide the flexibility and scalability required for modern data engineering tasks. This chapter introduced the basics of NoSQL, demonstrated how to use pymongo to interact with MongoDB, and explored indexing and querying techniques to optimize performance. In the next chapter, we'll dive into distributed data processing with tools like Apache Spark and PySpark.

Chapter 13: Distributed Data Processing with PySpark

Modern data engineering often involves working with massive datasets that require distributed systems for efficient processing. PySpark, the Python API for Apache Spark, provides a powerful framework for distributed data processing. This chapter introduces PySpark and its architecture, explores transforming data using RDDs and DataFrames, and discusses optimization techniques for improving performance.

1. Introduction to PySpark and the Spark Architecture

1.1. What is PySpark?

PySpark is the Python API for Apache Spark, an open-source distributed computing framework designed for large-scale data processing. PySpark enables data engineers to leverage Spark's scalability and efficiency using Python.

- **Core Features**:
    - Distributed processing across a cluster.
    - In-memory computation for faster processing.

- o Support for SQL queries, machine learning, and graph processing.

1.2. Spark Architecture

Apache Spark follows a master-worker architecture for distributed data processing.

- **Driver**:
  - o The central coordinator that schedules and monitors tasks.
  - o Runs the main application.
- **Cluster Manager**:
  - o Manages resources in the cluster (e.g., YARN, Mesos, or Spark Standalone).
- **Executors**:
  - o Perform distributed computations on worker nodes.
- **Resilient Distributed Dataset (RDD)**:
  - o Immutable, fault-tolerant collection of objects that can be operated on in parallel.

1.3. Installing PySpark

- Install PySpark.

bash

pip install pyspark

- Start a PySpark Shell:

bash

pyspark

---

2. Transforming Data with Spark RDDs and DataFrames

2.1. Working with RDDs

RDDs (Resilient Distributed Datasets) are the foundational data structure in Spark.

- **Creating RDDs**:

python

```
from pyspark import SparkContext

sc = SparkContext("local", "RDD Example")
data = [1, 2, 3, 4, 5]
rdd = sc.parallelize(data)
```

- **Transformations**: Transformations are lazy operations that define how data is processed.

o **Map**:

python

```
squared = rdd.map(lambda x: x ** 2)
print(squared.collect())  # Output: [1, 4, 9, 16, 25]
```

o **Filter**:

python

```
filtered = rdd.filter(lambda x: x > 2)
print(filtered.collect())  # Output: [3, 4, 5]
```

- **Actions**: Actions trigger the execution of transformations.
  o **Reduce**:

python

```
total = rdd.reduce(lambda x, y: x + y)
print(total)  # Output: 15
```

o **Collect**:

python

```
print(rdd.collect())  # Output: [1, 2, 3, 4, 5]
```

2.2. Working with DataFrames

DataFrames are a higher-level abstraction built on RDDs, optimized for SQL-like operations.

- **Creating DataFrames**:

python

from pyspark.sql import SparkSession

```
spark           =           SparkSession.builder.appName("DataFrame Example").getOrCreate()
data = [("Alice", 30), ("Bob", 25), ("Charlie", 35)]
df = spark.createDataFrame(data, ["Name", "Age"])
df.show()
```

Output:

diff

```
+-------+---+
|   Name|Age|
+-------+---+
|  Alice| 30|
|    Bob| 25|
|Charlie| 35|
+-------+---+
```

- **Transforming Data**:

python

```
df_filtered = df.filter(df.Age > 30)
df_filtered.show()
```

- **SQL Queries**:

python

```
df.createOrReplaceTempView("people")
spark.sql("SELECT * FROM people WHERE Age > 30").show()
```

2.3. Differences Between RDDs and DataFrames

Feature	RDDs	DataFrames
Abstraction	Low-level API	High-level API
Performance	Slower (no optimizations)	Faster (optimized execution)
Ease of Use	Requires more code	Simpler, SQL-like operations
Schema	No schema	Schema enforcement

3. Optimizing PySpark Jobs for Performance

Efficient PySpark jobs ensure faster execution and better resource utilization.

3.1. Use DataFrames Instead of RDDs

DataFrames are optimized using the Catalyst query optimizer, making them faster and easier to use.

3.2. Partitioning

Data is split into partitions for parallel processing.

- **Repartitioning**:

  python

  ```
  df_repartitioned = df.repartition(4)
  ```

- **Coalescing** (to reduce partitions):

  python

  ```
  df_coalesced = df.coalesce(2)
  ```

3.3. Persisting Data

Persisting data avoids recomputation of intermediate results.

- **Persist Data**:

python

```
from pyspark import StorageLevel

df.persist(StorageLevel.MEMORY_AND_DISK)
```

- **Unpersist Data**:

python

```
df.unpersist()
```

3.4. Caching

Caching stores intermediate results in memory for faster access.

- **Cache Data**:

python

```
df.cache()
```

3.5. Broadcast Variables

Broadcast variables allow sharing of small datasets across all nodes.

- **Using Broadcast Variables**:

python

```
broadcast_var = sc.broadcast([1, 2, 3])

def filter_func(x):
    return x in broadcast_var.value

rdd_filtered = rdd.filter(filter_func)
```

3.6. Avoid Shuffles

Shuffles occur during operations like groupBy or join, which can be costly.

- **Optimize Joins**: Use broadcast for small datasets:

    python

    ```
    from pyspark.sql.functions import broadcast

    joined_df = df1.join(broadcast(df2), "key")
    ```

4. Practical Example: Sales Data Analysis

Scenario: Analyze a large sales dataset using PySpark.

python

```
from pyspark.sql import SparkSession
```

```python
# Create a Spark session
spark = SparkSession.builder.appName("Sales Analysis").getOrCreate()

# Load data
sales_data = spark.read.csv("sales.csv", header=True, inferSchema=True)

# Filter data
filtered_sales = sales_data.filter(sales_data["Amount"] > 500)

# Group by and aggregate
sales_summary = filtered_sales.groupBy("Region").agg({"Amount": "sum"})
sales_summary.show()

# Optimize job with caching
sales_summary.cache()
sales_summary.count()  # Trigger caching
```

PySpark provides a powerful framework for distributed data processing, enabling efficient handling of large-scale datasets. By understanding the Spark architecture, leveraging RDDs and DataFrames for transformations, and optimizing jobs with partitioning, caching, and broadcast variables, you can build scalable and performant data pipelines. In the next chapter, we'll explore advanced data serialization and formats for efficient data storage and transfer.

Chapter 14: Data Serialization and Formats

Data serialization plays a crucial role in data engineering, allowing data to be efficiently stored, transferred, and processed. This chapter covers common serialization formats like JSON, XML, Parquet, and Avro, demonstrates reading and writing Parquet files using fastparquet, and guides you in choosing the right format for your data pipeline.

1. Understanding Data Serialization

Serialization converts data structures or objects into a format that can be easily stored or transmitted and later reconstructed.

1.1. Common Data Serialization Formats

1. **JSON (JavaScript Object Notation)**:
   - o **Structure**: Lightweight, human-readable text format.
   - o **Advantages**:
     - ▪ Easy to read and debug.
     - ▪ Widely supported in APIs and applications.
   - o **Disadvantages**:

- Can be verbose and inefficient for large datasets.

json

```
{
    "name": "Alice",
    "age": 30,
    "department": "Engineering"
}
```

2. XML (eXtensible Markup Language):

- o **Structure**: Markup-based, self-descriptive format.
- o **Advantages**:
  - Supports complex hierarchies.
  - Schema validation.
- o **Disadvantages**:
  - Verbose and harder to parse than JSON.

xml

```
<employee>
    <name>Alice</name>
    <age>30</age>
    <department>Engineering</department>
</employee>
```

3. Parquet:

- o **Structure**: Columnar storage format optimized for analytical queries.
- o **Advantages**:
  - High compression efficiency.
  - Faster read/write for columnar data.
- o **Disadvantages**:
  - Harder to work with in non-analytical scenarios.

4. **Avro**:
   - o **Structure**: Binary row-based format with a schema.
   - o **Advantages**:
     - Compact and efficient.
     - Supports schema evolution.
   - o **Disadvantages**:
     - Less human-readable.

1.2. Choosing a Format Based on Use Case

Use Case	Recommended Format
Human-readable storage	JSON, XML
Efficient analytics	Parquet
Streaming and messaging	Avro

Use Case	Recommended Format
Hierarchical data	XML

2. Reading and Writing Parquet Files with fastparquet

Parquet is a popular format for big data systems, especially for columnar storage. The fastparquet library is a fast and efficient tool for working with Parquet files in Python.

2.1. Installing fastparquet

- Install fastparquet:

bash

```
pip install fastparquet
```

2.2. Writing Data to Parquet

- **Using pandas with fastparquet:**

python

```
import pandas as pd

data = {
```

```
    "Name": ["Alice", "Bob", "Charlie"],
    "Age": [30, 25, 35],
    "Salary": [75000, 50000, 80000]
}

df = pd.DataFrame(data)

# Save to Parquet
df.to_parquet("employees.parquet", engine="fastparquet", index=False)
```

2.3. Reading Parquet Files

- **Read with pandas**:

  python

  ```
  # Read Parquet file
  df = pd.read_parquet("employees.parquet", engine="fastparquet")
  print(df)
  ```

2.4. Working with Large Datasets

Parquet's columnar structure is ideal for large datasets.

- **Filtering Columns**:

  python

```python
df    =    pd.read_parquet("employees.parquet",    columns=["Name",
"Salary"])
```

- **Appending to Existing Files**:

python

```python
df_new = pd.DataFrame({"Name": ["Diana"], "Age": [28], "Salary":
[65000]})
df_new.to_parquet("employees.parquet",          engine="fastparquet",
append=True)
```

2.5. Parquet vs. Other Formats

Feature	JSON	XML	Parquet	Avro
Human-readable	Yes	Yes	No	No
Compression Efficiency	Low	Low	High	Medium
Analytical Performance	Poor	Poor	Excellent	Good
Schema Validation	No	Yes	No (optional)	Yes

3. Choosing the Right Data Format for Your Pipeline

Selecting the best data format depends on the specific needs of your pipeline.

3.1. Factors to Consider

1. **Data Volume**:
   - o For small datasets: JSON or XML.
   - o For large datasets: Parquet or Avro.
2. **Read/Write Frequency**:
   - o High frequency: Parquet (optimized for quick reads).
3. **Use Case**:
   - o Analytics: Parquet for columnar efficiency.
   - o Data exchange: JSON for compatibility.

3.2. Practical Guidelines

- **Use JSON**:
  - o For APIs or when human readability is important.
- **Use XML**:
  - o For hierarchical data or schema enforcement.
- **Use Parquet**:
  - o For big data analytics and columnar storage.
- **Use Avro**:
  - o For streaming or messaging systems with schema evolution.

4. Practical Example: Storing and Querying Sales Data

Scenario: Store sales data in Parquet format for efficient querying and analysis.

python

```python
import pandas as pd

# Create sales data
sales_data = {
    "OrderID": [1, 2, 3, 4],
    "Customer": ["Alice", "Bob", "Charlie", "Diana"],
    "Amount": [100, 150, 200, 250],
    "Region": ["North", "South", "East", "West"]
}
sales_df = pd.DataFrame(sales_data)

# Save to Parquet
sales_df.to_parquet("sales.parquet", engine="fastparquet", index=False)

# Read Parquet file
sales_df = pd.read_parquet("sales.parquet", engine="fastparquet")

# Filter and analyze data
north_sales = sales_df[sales_df["Region"] == "North"]
print(north_sales)
```

Data serialization is a critical step in data engineering pipelines, enabling efficient storage and transfer of data. Understanding when to use formats like JSON, XML, Parquet, and Avro ensures your pipeline is optimized for both performance and usability. By leveraging libraries like fastparquet, you can work seamlessly with Parquet files for analytics and big data processing. In the next chapter, we'll explore handling streaming data and real-time processing pipelines.

Chapter 15: Message Queues and Streaming Data

In modern data engineering, handling real-time data streams is crucial for applications like event monitoring, log processing, and real-time analytics. Message queues and streaming systems like RabbitMQ and Apache Kafka are at the core of these processes. This chapter introduces message queues, demonstrates how to work with Apache Kafka in Python, and covers real-time data processing with kafka-python and Spark Streaming.

---

1. Introduction to Message Queues (RabbitMQ, Kafka)

1.1. What Are Message Queues?

Message queues facilitate asynchronous communication between components of a system by passing messages through a queue. This ensures that producers and consumers can operate independently.

- **Key Features**:
    - Asynchronous communication.
    - Decoupled systems.
    - Fault tolerance and durability.

1.2. RabbitMQ

RabbitMQ is a lightweight, open-source message broker.

- **Features**:
    - Uses AMQP (Advanced Message Queuing Protocol).
    - Supports various exchange types (direct, fanout, topic).
    - Easy to configure and deploy.
- **Use Cases**:
    - Task queues.
    - Decoupling services in microservice architectures.

1.3. Apache Kafka

Apache Kafka is a distributed event-streaming platform designed for high-throughput and fault-tolerant data pipelines.

- **Features**:
    - Durable storage with replication.
    - High throughput for large-scale systems.
    - Real-time event processing.
- **Use Cases**:
    - Log aggregation.
    - Real-time analytics.

- o Event sourcing.

1.4. RabbitMQ vs. Kafka

Feature	RabbitMQ	Apache Kafka
Protocol	AMQP	Custom protocol
Persistence	Message queues	Topic-based storage
Scalability	Moderate	High
Use Case	Task queues, microservices	Event streams, analytics

---

2. Working with Apache Kafka in Python

2.1. Setting Up Kafka

1. **Download Kafka**:
   - o Download Kafka.
   - o Extract the files.
2. **Start Kafka**:
   - o Start ZooKeeper:

     bash

```
bin/zookeeper-server-start.sh config/zookeeper.properties
```

- ○ Start Kafka server:

```bash
bash
```

```
bin/kafka-server-start.sh config/server.properties
```

2.2. Installing kafka-python

Install the Kafka client library for Python:

```bash
bash
```

```
pip install kafka-python
```

2.3. Creating a Kafka Producer

A Kafka producer publishes messages to a topic.

```python
python
```

```python
from kafka import KafkaProducer

producer = KafkaProducer(bootstrap_servers='localhost:9092')

# Send a message
producer.send('test-topic', b'Hello, Kafka!')
producer.close()
```

2.4. Creating a Kafka Consumer

A Kafka consumer reads messages from a topic.

python

```
from kafka import KafkaConsumer

consumer = KafkaConsumer(
    'test-topic',
    bootstrap_servers='localhost:9092',
    auto_offset_reset='earliest'
)

# Read messages
for message in consumer:
    print(f"Received: {message.value.decode('utf-8')}")
```

2.5. Managing Kafka Topics

- **Create a Topic**:

  bash

  ```
  bin/kafka-topics.sh --create --topic test-topic --bootstrap-server localhost:9092 --partitions 1 --replication-factor 1
  ```

- **List Topics**:

  bash

bin/kafka-topics.sh --list --bootstrap-server localhost:9092

- **Delete a Topic**:

bash

bin/kafka-topics.sh   --delete   --topic   test-topic   --bootstrap-server localhost:9092

3. Real-Time Data Processing with Kafka and Spark Streaming

3.1. Introduction to Spark Streaming

Spark Streaming processes real-time data streams using Spark's distributed architecture. It integrates seamlessly with Kafka.

3.2. Setting Up Spark Streaming with Kafka

1. **Install Spark and PySpark**:

bash

pip install pyspark

2. **Install Spark-Kafka Integration**: Include the Kafka integration package when starting Spark:

bash

```
spark-submit    --packages    org.apache.spark:spark-sql-kafka-0-
10_2.12:3.3.1 your_script.py
```

3.3. Example: Real-Time Word Count from Kafka

- **Kafka Producer**:

python

```python
from kafka import KafkaProducer
import time

producer = KafkaProducer(bootstrap_servers='localhost:9092')
messages = ["hello world", "real-time processing", "data engineering"]

for msg in messages:
    producer.send('word-count-topic', msg.encode('utf-8'))
    time.sleep(2)
producer.close()
```

- **Spark Streaming Application**:

python

```python
from pyspark.sql import SparkSession
from pyspark.sql.functions import explode, split
```

```
spark                                                    =
SparkSession.builder.appName("KafkaWordCount").getOrCreate()

# Read data from Kafka
df = spark.readStream.format("kafka") \
    .option("kafka.bootstrap.servers", "localhost:9092") \
    .option("subscribe", "word-count-topic") \
    .load()

# Extract and process messages
messages = df.selectExpr("CAST(value AS STRING)")

# Split messages into words
words      =      messages.select(explode(split(messages.value,      "
")).alias("word"))

# Count words
word_counts = words.groupBy("word").count()

# Write results to console
query                                                    =
word_counts.writeStream.outputMode("complete").format("console").s
tart()
query.awaitTermination()
```

3.4. Optimizing Real-Time Processing

- **Batch Interval**: Choose an appropriate batch interval to balance latency and throughput.

python

```
spark.readStream.option("maxOffsetsPerTrigger", 1000)
```

- **Checkpointing**: Enable checkpointing to ensure fault tolerance.

python

```
query = word_counts.writeStream \
    .outputMode("complete") \
    .format("console") \
    .option("checkpointLocation", "/path/to/checkpoint") \
    .start()
```

- **Use Kafka Partitions**: Distribute load across Kafka partitions for better parallelism.

---

4. Practical Example: Real-Time Sales Dashboard

Scenario: Process real-time sales data from Kafka and display aggregated metrics.

1. **Kafka Producer**: Send sales data to Kafka:

python

```
sales_data = [
    {"region": "North", "sales": 100},
```

```python
    {"region": "South", "sales": 150}
]
for sale in sales_data:
    producer.send('sales-topic', json.dumps(sale).encode('utf-8'))
```

2. **Spark Streaming Application**: Process and aggregate sales data:

python

```python
sales_df = spark.readStream.format("kafka") \
    .option("kafka.bootstrap.servers", "localhost:9092") \
    .option("subscribe", "sales-topic") \
    .load()

sales_data = sales_df.selectExpr("CAST(value AS STRING)")
sales_json      =      sales_data.select(from_json(sales_data.value,
schema).alias("data"))

aggregated_sales                                                  =
sales_json.groupBy("region").agg(sum("sales").alias("total_sales"))

query                                                             =
aggregated_sales.writeStream.outputMode("complete").format("consol
e").start()
query.awaitTermination()
```

Message queues and streaming platforms like RabbitMQ and Apache Kafka are integral to real-time data engineering workflows. PySpark's Streaming API provides a robust solution for processing and analyzing streaming data. By combining Kafka with Spark Streaming, data engineers can build scalable, fault-tolerant pipelines for real-time analytics. In the next chapter, we'll explore advanced data visualization techniques and tools.

Chapter 16: APIs for Data Engineering

APIs (Application Programming Interfaces) are essential for integrating data pipelines, enabling communication between applications, and exposing data for consumption. This chapter covers building RESTful APIs with Flask, integrating data pipelines with APIs, and implementing error handling and logging for robust API-based workflows.

1. Building RESTful APIs with Flask

1.1. What is Flask?

Flask is a lightweight Python web framework that simplifies building RESTful APIs. It is highly extensible and ideal for small to medium-scale applications.

1.2. Installing Flask

Install Flask using pip:

bash

pip install flask

1.3. Creating a Basic API

- **Hello World API**:

python

```
from flask import Flask

app = Flask(__name__)

@app.route('/api/hello', methods=['GET'])
def hello_world():
    return {"message": "Hello, World!"}

if __name__ == '__main__':
    app.run(debug=True)
```

- **Running the API**: Save the file as app.py and run:

bash

```
python app.py
```
Access the API at http://127.0.0.1:5000/api/hello.

1.4. API with Dynamic Parameters

- **Endpoint with Query Parameters**:

python

```python
@app.route('/api/square', methods=['GET'])
def square():
    number = int(request.args.get('number', 0))
    return {"number": number, "square": number ** 2}
```

Example request: http://127.0.0.1:5000/api/square?number=4

1.5. CRUD Operations

Create, Read, Update, and Delete operations form the backbone of most RESTful APIs.

- **Example**: Employee Management API:

python

```python
employees = []

@app.route('/api/employees', methods=['POST'])
def add_employee():
    data = request.json
    employees.append(data)
    return {"message": "Employee added successfully!"}, 201

@app.route('/api/employees', methods=['GET'])
def get_employees():
```

```
    return {"employees": employees}

@app.route('/api/employees/<int:id>', methods=['PUT'])
def update_employee(id):
    data = request.json
    employees[id] = data
    return {"message": "Employee updated successfully!"}

@app.route('/api/employees/<int:id>', methods=['DELETE'])
def delete_employee(id):
    employees.pop(id)
    return {"message": "Employee deleted successfully!"}
```

2. Integrating Data Pipelines with APIs

2.1. Consuming External APIs in Data Pipelines

Use Python's requests library to integrate APIs into your pipelines.

- **Example**: Fetching data from an API and storing it in a database:

python

```python
import requests
import pandas as pd
from sqlalchemy import create_engine

# Fetch data from API
```

```python
response = requests.get('https://api.example.com/data')
data = response.json()

# Convert to DataFrame
df = pd.DataFrame(data)

# Save to database
engine = create_engine('sqlite:///example.db')
df.to_sql('api_data', engine, if_exists='replace', index=False)
```

2.2. Exposing Data Pipelines via APIs

Expose the results of your data pipelines as RESTful APIs.

- **Example**: Query a database and return results via an API:

  python

  ```python
  from flask import jsonify
  import pandas as pd
  from sqlalchemy import create_engine

  engine = create_engine('sqlite:///example.db')

  @app.route('/api/data', methods=['GET'])
  def get_data():
      query = "SELECT * FROM api_data"
      df = pd.read_sql(query, engine)
      return jsonify(df.to_dict(orient='records'))
  ```

2.3. Real-Time Data Processing with APIs

Integrate streaming data into APIs for real-time updates.

- **Example**: Stream data from Kafka to an API endpoint:

python

```python
from kafka import KafkaConsumer

consumer = KafkaConsumer(
    'real-time-topic',
    bootstrap_servers='localhost:9092',
    auto_offset_reset='earliest'
)

@app.route('/api/stream', methods=['GET'])
def stream_data():
    messages = []
    for message in consumer:
        messages.append(message.value.decode('utf-8'))
        if len(messages) >= 10:  # Send 10 messages at a time
            break
    return {"messages": messages}
```

3. Error Handling and Logging in API-Based Workflows

3.1. Implementing Error Handling

Error handling ensures your API can gracefully respond to unexpected issues.

- **Using try and except:**

python

```python
@app.route('/api/divide', methods=['GET'])
def divide():
    try:
        a = int(request.args.get('a'))
        b = int(request.args.get('b'))
        return {"result": a / b}
    except ZeroDivisionError:
        return {"error": "Division by zero is not allowed!"}, 400
    except Exception as e:
        return {"error": str(e)}, 500
```

- **Custom Error Handlers:**

python

```python
@app.errorhandler(404)
def not_found_error(error):
    return {"error": "Endpoint not found"}, 404


@app.errorhandler(500)
def internal_error(error):
    return {"error": "Internal server error"}, 500
```

3.2. Logging

Logging helps debug issues and monitor API performance.

- **Setting Up Logging**:

python

import logging

logging.basicConfig(level=logging.INFO)

```
@app.route('/api/log', methods=['GET'])
def log_example():
    logging.info("Log example endpoint called")
    return {"message": "Check logs for details"}
```

- **Writing Logs to a File**:

python

logging.basicConfig(filename='app.log', level=logging.DEBUG)

- **Logging Errors**:

python

```
try:
    1 / 0
except ZeroDivisionError as e:
    logging.error("Error occurred: %s", e)
```

3.3. Monitoring APIs

Use tools like Prometheus or Grafana to monitor API performance and usage metrics.

4. Practical Example: Employee Management API with Logging

python

```python
from flask import Flask, request, jsonify
import logging

app = Flask(__name__)
logging.basicConfig(level=logging.INFO)

employees = []

@app.route('/api/employees', methods=['POST'])
def add_employee():
    try:
        data = request.json
        employees.append(data)
        logging.info("Employee added: %s", data)
        return {"message": "Employee added successfully!"}, 201
    except Exception as e:
        logging.error("Error adding employee: %s", e)
        return {"error": "Failed to add employee"}, 500
```

```python
@app.route('/api/employees', methods=['GET'])
def get_employees():
    logging.info("Fetching employees")
    return jsonify(employees)


@app.route('/api/employees/<int:id>', methods=['DELETE'])
def delete_employee(id):
    try:
        employee = employees.pop(id)
        logging.info("Employee deleted: %s", employee)
        return {"message": "Employee deleted successfully!"}
    except IndexError:
        logging.error("Employee not found: ID %d", id)
        return {"error": "Employee not found"}, 404


if __name__ == '__main__':
    app.run(debug=True)
```

APIs are indispensable in modern data engineering workflows, enabling integration and communication between components. By building robust RESTful APIs with Flask, integrating APIs into data pipelines, and implementing error handling and logging, you can create reliable and maintainable workflows. In the next chapter, we'll explore cloud platforms for data storage and processing.

Chapter 17: Cloud Computing for Data Engineering

Cloud computing has revolutionized the way data engineers store, process, and analyze data. Platforms like AWS, GCP, and Azure provide scalable, flexible, and cost-efficient solutions for data engineering tasks. This chapter introduces popular cloud platforms, explores using Python with AWS services like S3, Lambda, and DynamoDB, and demonstrates how to deploy data engineering pipelines in the cloud.

1. Introduction to Cloud Platforms (AWS, GCP, Azure)

1.1. What is Cloud Computing?

Cloud computing provides on-demand access to computing resources such as servers, storage, and databases over the internet. It eliminates the need for maintaining physical infrastructure.

- **Key Benefits**:
    - o **Scalability**: Scale resources up or down as needed.
    - o **Cost Efficiency**: Pay for only what you use.

o **Global Accessibility**: Access resources from anywhere.

1.2. Overview of Popular Cloud Platforms

Feature	AWS	GCP	Azure
Storage	S3	Cloud Storage	Azure Blob Storage
Compute	EC2, Lambda	Compute Engine, Cloud Functions	Virtual Machines, Azure Functions
Database Services	RDS, DynamoDB	BigQuery, Firestore	SQL Database, Cosmos DB
Data Processing	EMR, Glue	Dataflow, Dataproc	Synapse Analytics

2. Using Python with AWS (S3, Lambda, DynamoDB)

2.1. AWS Setup

1. **Create an AWS Account**:

   o Sign up at aws.amazon.com.

2. **Install AWS CLI**:

bash

```
pip install awscli
aws configure
```

3. **Install boto3**: AWS SDK for Python:

bash

```
pip install boto3
```

2.2. Working with S3

Amazon S3 (Simple Storage Service) is a scalable storage solution for data engineering tasks.

- **Upload and Download Files**:

python

```
import boto3

s3 = boto3.client('s3')

# Upload a file
s3.upload_file('local_file.txt', 'bucket_name', 'remote_file.txt')

# Download a file
```

```
s3.download_file('bucket_name', 'remote_file.txt', 'local_file.txt')
```

- **List Buckets and Objects**:

python

```python
# List buckets
buckets = s3.list_buckets()
for bucket in buckets['Buckets']:
    print(bucket['Name'])

# List objects in a bucket
objects = s3.list_objects(Bucket='bucket_name')
for obj in objects['Contents']:
    print(obj['Key'])
```

2.3. Using Lambda Functions

AWS Lambda is a serverless compute service for running code in response to events.

- **Create a Lambda Function**:
    1. Write your function:

python

```python
def lambda_handler(event, context):
    return {"message": "Hello from Lambda!"}
```

2. Zip and upload your function to AWS Lambda via the console or AWS CLI.

- **Invoke a Lambda Function**:

python

```python
lambda_client = boto3.client('lambda')

response = lambda_client.invoke(
    FunctionName='my_lambda_function',
    Payload=b'{"key": "value"}'
)
print(response['Payload'].read().decode())
```

2.4. Using DynamoDB

Amazon DynamoDB is a NoSQL database for storing key-value and document data.

- **Create a Table**:

python

```python
dynamodb = boto3.resource('dynamodb')

table = dynamodb.create_table(
    TableName='employees',
    KeySchema=[
        {'AttributeName': 'id', 'KeyType': 'HASH'}  # Partition key
```

```
        ],
        AttributeDefinitions=[
            {'AttributeName': 'id', 'AttributeType': 'S'}
        ],
        ProvisionedThroughput={
            'ReadCapacityUnits': 5,
            'WriteCapacityUnits': 5
        }
    )
    table.wait_until_exists()
```

- **Insert and Retrieve Data**:

python

```
table = dynamodb.Table('employees')

# Insert data
table.put_item(Item={'id':    '123',    'name':    'Alice',    'department':
'Engineering'})

# Retrieve data
response = table.get_item(Key={'id': '123'})
print(response['Item'])
```

3. Deploying Data Engineering Pipelines on the Cloud

3.1. Deploying ETL Pipelines with AWS Glue

AWS Glue is a fully managed ETL service for data preparation and transformation.

- **Steps**:
    1. Create a Glue job in the AWS Management Console.
    2. Write a Python script to extract, transform, and load data.
    3. Execute the job on a schedule or trigger it via an event.

3.2. Orchestrating Pipelines with AWS Step Functions

AWS Step Functions enable orchestration of multiple services in a pipeline.

- **Example**: ETL pipeline with S3, Lambda, and DynamoDB:
    1. Upload raw data to S3.
    2. Trigger a Lambda function to process the data.
    3. Store processed data in DynamoDB.

3.3. Building Serverless Pipelines

Serverless architectures reduce operational overhead.

- **Example**:

- o   Use AWS Lambda to process streaming data from an S3 event.
- o   Store results in DynamoDB for quick access.

3.4. Monitoring and Logging

- **CloudWatch**: Monitor metrics and logs for your pipelines.

  python

```python
logs = boto3.client('logs')

response = logs.get_log_events(
    logGroupName='my-log-group',
    logStreamName='my-log-stream'
)
for event in response['events']:
    print(event['message'])
```

4. Practical Example: End-to-End Pipeline on AWS

Scenario: Process sales data uploaded to S3, analyze it using Lambda, and store results in DynamoDB.

1. **Step 1: S3 Upload**: Upload raw sales data to an S3 bucket.
2. **Step 2: Lambda Processing**:
   - o   Trigger a Lambda function on S3 upload.
   - o   Parse, filter, and aggregate sales data.

o Store the results in DynamoDB.

python

```python
def lambda_handler(event, context):
    import boto3
    import json

    s3 = boto3.client('s3')
    dynamodb = boto3.resource('dynamodb')
    table = dynamodb.Table('sales_data')

    # Get file from S3
    bucket = event['Records'][0]['s3']['bucket']['name']
    key = event['Records'][0]['s3']['object']['key']
    response = s3.get_object(Bucket=bucket, Key=key)
    data = json.loads(response['Body'].read())

    # Process and store data in DynamoDB
    for record in data:
        table.put_item(Item=record)

    return {"message": "Data processed and stored successfully"}
```

3. **Step 3: Analyze with DynamoDB**: Query processed data from DynamoDB for reporting.

Cloud computing simplifies data engineering by providing scalable and reliable platforms for storage, computation, and processing. By leveraging AWS services like S3, Lambda, and DynamoDB, you can build powerful and efficient data pipelines. In the next chapter, we'll explore data governance and security in data engineering workflows.

Chapter 18: Introduction to Docker and Kubernetes

Containerization has transformed the way applications are built, deployed, and managed. Docker enables you to package applications and their dependencies into portable containers, while Kubernetes orchestrates containerized workflows at scale. This chapter introduces Docker, demonstrates how to create Docker images for Python applications, and explores Kubernetes for managing workflows.

1. Basics of Containerization with Docker

1.1. What is Docker?

Docker is a platform for creating, deploying, and running applications in isolated environments called containers.

- **Key Features**:
  - Portability: "Write once, run anywhere."
  - Lightweight: Containers share the host OS kernel.
  - Efficiency: Fast startup times compared to virtual machines.

1.2. Installing Docker

1. Download Docker Desktop from docker.com.
2. Install and verify:

bash

docker --version

1.3. Key Docker Concepts

- **Images**: Read-only templates used to create containers.
- **Containers**: Running instances of images.
- **Dockerfile**: A script to define how an image is built.
- **Docker Hub**: A repository for sharing images.

1.4. Basic Docker Commands

- **Pull an Image**:

bash

docker pull python:3.9

- **Run a Container**:

bash

docker run -it --name my_python_container python:3.9

- **List Running Containers**:

  bash

  docker ps

- **Stop a Container**:

  bash

  docker stop my_python_container

- **Remove a Container**:

  bash

  docker rm my_python_container

---

2. Creating Docker Images for Python Applications

2.1. Writing a Dockerfile

A Dockerfile defines the environment and dependencies for your application.

- **Example: Flask Application**:

    1. Create a Dockerfile:

        dockerfile

        ```
        # Use a base image
        FROM python:3.9-slim

        # Set the working directory
        WORKDIR /app

        # Copy application files
        COPY requirements.txt requirements.txt
        COPY app.py app.py

        # Install dependencies
        RUN pip install -r requirements.txt

        # Expose the port
        EXPOSE 5000

        # Run the application
        CMD ["python", "app.py"]
        ```

    2. Create requirements.txt:

        flask

    3. Create app.py:

python

```python
from flask import Flask

app = Flask(__name__)

@app.route('/')
def home():
    return "Hello, Docker!"

if __name__ == '__main__':
    app.run(host='0.0.0.0', port=5000)
```

2.2. Building and Running the Docker Image

1. **Build the Image**:

   bash

   ```bash
   docker build -t flask-app .
   ```

2. **Run the Container**:

   bash

   ```bash
   docker run -p 5000:5000 flask-app
   ```

3. **Access the Application**: Open http://localhost:5000 in your browser.

2.3. Publishing the Image

1. **Tag the Image**:

   bash

   docker tag flask-app your_dockerhub_username/flask-app

2. **Push to Docker Hub**:

   bash

   docker push your_dockerhub_username/flask-app

3. Orchestrating Workflows with Kubernetes

3.1. What is Kubernetes?

Kubernetes (K8s) is an open-source platform for automating deployment, scaling, and management of containerized applications.

- **Key Features**:
  - Scaling: Automatically adjusts resources based on load.
  - High Availability: Ensures applications remain available during failures.

o Load Balancing: Distributes traffic across containers.

3.2. Setting Up Kubernetes

1. **Install Minikube**: Minikube is a local Kubernetes cluster:

bash

```
brew install minikube
minikube start
```

2. **Install kubectl**: Kubernetes command-line tool:

bash

```
brew install kubectl
kubectl version --client
```

3.3. Key Kubernetes Concepts

- **Pods**: Smallest deployable unit, typically a single container.
- **Deployments**: Manage updates and scaling for Pods.
- **Services**: Expose Pods to external traffic.

3.4. Deploying a Python Application

- **Create a Deployment**:

1. Create deployment.yaml:

yaml

```yaml
apiVersion: apps/v1
kind: Deployment
metadata:
  name: flask-app
spec:
  replicas: 2
  selector:
    matchLabels:
      app: flask-app
  template:
    metadata:
      labels:
        app: flask-app
    spec:
      containers:
      - name: flask-app
        image: your_dockerhub_username/flask-app
        ports:
        - containerPort: 5000
```

2. Apply the Deployment:

bash

```bash
kubectl apply -f deployment.yaml
```

- **Expose the Deployment**:

1. Create service.yaml:

yaml

```
apiVersion: v1
kind: Service
metadata:
  name: flask-service
spec:
  selector:
    app: flask-app
  ports:
  - protocol: TCP
    port: 80
    targetPort: 5000
  type: LoadBalancer
```

2. Apply the Service:

bash

```
kubectl apply -f service.yaml
```

3.5. Scaling Applications

- **Scale a Deployment**:

bash

```
kubectl scale deployment flask-app --replicas=5
```

- **View Logs**:

  bash

  kubectl logs <pod-name>

3.6. Monitoring and Debugging

- **Check Cluster Status**:

  bash

  kubectl get pods
  kubectl get services

- **Describe Resources**:

  bash

  kubectl describe pcd <pod-name>

---

4. Practical Example: End-to-End Workflow

Scenario: Deploy a Python Flask app using Docker and Kubernetes.

1. **Build Docker Image**:

   bash

   docker build -t flask-app .

2. **Push to Docker Hub**:

bash

docker push your_dockerhub_username/flask-app

3. **Create Kubernetes Deployment and Service**: Apply the deployment.yaml and service.yaml files.

4. **Access the Application**: Use the external IP provided by the Kubernetes service:

bash

kubectl get services

Docker and Kubernetes provide a powerful foundation for containerization and orchestration in data engineering workflows. Docker simplifies the packaging and deployment of applications, while Kubernetes ensures scalability, reliability, and efficient resource management. By mastering these tools, data engineers can build robust and scalable pipelines for modern data applications. In the next chapter, we'll explore best practices for data governance and security in engineering workflows.

Chapter 19: Data Security and Privacy

As data becomes a critical asset, ensuring its security and maintaining privacy are essential for data engineering workflows. This chapter explores methods for protecting sensitive data, implementing encryption and secure data transfer, and adhering to regulatory requirements like GDPR and CCPA.

1. Protecting Sensitive Data

1.1. Understanding Sensitive Data

Sensitive data includes personally identifiable information (PII), financial records, health information, and proprietary business data.

- **Examples**:
    - PII: Names, addresses, social security numbers.
    - Financial Data: Credit card numbers, account details.
    - Health Data: Patient records under HIPAA.

1.2. Data Masking

Mask sensitive information in datasets for testing or analysis.

- **Static Masking**: Replace sensitive data with fictitious values in a static dataset.

python

import pandas as pd

```
data = pd.DataFrame({'Name': ['Alice', 'Bob'], 'SSN': ['123-45-6789',
'987-65-4321']})
data['SSN'] = data['SSN'].apply(lambda x: 'XXX-XX-' + x[-4:])
print(data)
```

- **Dynamic Masking**: Apply masking rules during runtime, e.g., only show the last four digits of a credit card.

1.3. Access Controls

Restrict access to sensitive data based on roles and permissions.

- **Best Practices**:
  - Implement role-based access control (RBAC).
  - Use principles like least privilege and need-to-know access.
  - Monitor access logs for anomalies.

1.4. Data Anonymization

Anonymize data to prevent identification of individuals.

- **Example**: Replace unique identifiers with pseudonyms or generalize data fields.

python

```
data['Name'] = data['Name'].apply(lambda x: 'User_' + str(hash(x) % 1000))
```

2. Implementing Encryption and Secure Data Transfer

2.1. Data Encryption

Encryption transforms data into unreadable formats to protect it during storage and transit.

2.2. Types of Encryption

1. **Symmetric Encryption**:
   o Uses the same key for encryption and decryption.
   o Example: AES (Advanced Encryption Standard).

python

```
from cryptography.fernet import Fernet
```

```
key = Fernet.generate_key()
cipher = Fernet(key)

encrypted = cipher.encrypt(b"Sensitive data")
decrypted = cipher.decrypt(encrypted)

print(f"Encrypted: {encrypted}")
print(f"Decrypted: {decrypted.decode()}")
```

2. **Asymmetric Encryption**:

   o Uses a public key for encryption and a private key for decryption.

   o Example: RSA (Rivest-Shamir-Adleman).

2.3. Secure Data Transfer

Ensure data is encrypted during transfer to prevent interception.

- **Transport Layer Security (TLS)**: Encrypt data in transit using HTTPS, FTPS, or SSH.

  bash

  ```bash
  scp -i private_key.pem file.txt user@remote_server:/path/to/destination
  ```

- **Virtual Private Network (VPN)**: Use a VPN for secure communication over public networks.

2.4. Encrypting Data at Rest

Encrypt stored data to prevent unauthorized access.

- **Example**: Enable encryption in cloud services like AWS S3:

```bash
aws s3api put-bucket-encryption \
  --bucket my-bucket \
  --server-side-encryption-configuration
'{"Rules":[{"ApplyServerSideEncryptionByDefault":{"SSEAlgorithm"
:"AES256"}}]}'
```

3. Best Practices for Ensuring Compliance with GDPR/CCPA

3.1. Overview of GDPR and CCPA

1. **GDPR (General Data Protection Regulation)**:
   - EU regulation for data protection and privacy.
   - Key principles:
     - Right to access, rectify, and erase personal data.
     - Data minimization and purpose limitation.
     - Explicit user consent for data collection.

2. **CCPA (California Consumer Privacy Act)**:
   - Provides California residents with rights to control their personal data.
   - Key principles:
     - Right to know what data is collected.
     - Right to opt out of data selling.
     - Right to delete personal data.

3.2. Data Privacy Compliance

1. **Data Mapping**:
   - Identify where personal data is collected, processed, and stored.
2. **User Consent**:
   - Obtain explicit consent for data collection and processing.
   - Example: GDPR-compliant cookie banners.
3. **Data Minimization**:
   - Collect only necessary data.

python

```
# Example: Only collect essential fields
user_data = {"name": "Alice", "email": "alice@example.com"}
```

4. **Audit Trails**:

o Maintain records of data access and processing activities.

5. **Data Breach Response**:

o Notify affected users and authorities within 72 hours (GDPR requirement).

3.3. Implementing the Right to Erasure

Allow users to delete their personal data upon request.

- **Example**:

python

```
def delete_user_data(user_id):
    # Simulate data deletion
    database.delete({"user_id": user_id})
    return {"message": "User data deleted"}
```

3.4. Privacy by Design

Embed privacy measures into the architecture of data systems.

- **Examples**:
    o Encrypt sensitive fields in databases.
    o Use pseudonymization for analytics.

4. Practical Example: End-to-End Secure Data Pipeline

Scenario: Build a secure data pipeline for storing customer data.

1. **Step 1: Collect Data with Consent**:
   - o Use a web form that explicitly requests user consent.
2. **Step 2: Encrypt Data in Transit**:
   - o Use HTTPS for API endpoints.

python

```python
@app.route('/submit', methods=['POST'])
def submit_data():
    encrypted_data = cipher.encrypt(request.json['data'].encode())
    return {"message": "Data received securely"}
```

3. **Step 3: Store Data Securely**:
   - o Encrypt sensitive fields before saving them to a database.

python

```python
encrypted_name = cipher.encrypt("Alice".encode())
database.insert({"name": encrypted_name})
```

4. **Step 4: Enable Right to Erasure**:
   - o Implement an API endpoint to delete user data.

python

```
@app.route('/delete/<user_id>', methods=['DELETE'])
def delete_data(user_id):
    database.delete({"user_id": user_id})
    return {"message": "Data deleted"}
```

5. **Step 5: Audit Data Access**:
   o Log all data access activities for auditing.

Data security and privacy are critical components of data engineering. By protecting sensitive data, implementing encryption, and adhering to GDPR/CCPA requirements, you can build secure and compliant data pipelines. The principles covered in this chapter ensure data remains safe while respecting user privacy. In the next chapter, we'll explore advanced analytics and machine learning integration in data engineering workflows.

Chapter 20: Testing and Debugging Data Pipelines

Testing and debugging are critical to building reliable and robust data pipelines. This chapter covers using pytest for unit testing, debugging Python scripts and pipelines, and implementing automated testing strategies to ensure pipeline reliability.

1. Unit Testing with pytest

1.1. What is Unit Testing?

Unit testing involves verifying individual components or functions of a data pipeline to ensure they work as expected.

1.2. Setting Up pytest

1. Install pytest:

    bash

    pip install pytest

2. Create a test file:

   o Test files should start with test_ or end with _test.py.

   o Example: test_pipeline.py.

1.3. Writing Unit Tests

- **Example: Testing a Transformation Function**:

python

```
# transformations.py
def clean_data(data):
    return [x.strip().lower() for x in data if x]


# test_transformations.py
from transformations import clean_data

def test_clean_data():
    input_data = [" Alice ", "Bob", None, " Charlie "]
    expected = ["alice", "bob", "charlie"]
    assert clean_data(input_data) == expected
```

- **Run Tests**:

bash

```
pytest test_transformations.py
```

1.4. Using pytest Fixtures

Fixtures provide pre-defined setups for tests.

- **Example**: Mocking Input Data

```python
import pytest

@pytest.fixture
def sample_data():
    return [" Alice ", "Bob", None, "  Charlie  "]

def test_clean_data(sample_data):
    from transformations import clean_data
    expected = ["alice", "bob", "charlie"]
    assert clean_data(sample_data) == expected
```

1.5. Parameterized Tests

Test multiple input-output pairs efficiently.

- **Example**:

```python
import pytest
from transformations import clean_data
```

```python
@pytest.mark.parametrize("input_data,expected", [
    ([" Alice "], ["alice"]),
    ([" Bob ", None], ["bob"]),
    ([], []),
])
def test_clean_data(input_data, expected):
    assert clean_data(input_data) == expected
```

---

2. Debugging Python Scripts and Pipelines

2.1. Common Debugging Tools

1. **print() Statements**:
   o Quickly inspect variable values.

python

```python
print(f"Debugging: {variable}")
```

2. **Using a Debugger**:
   o Built-in Python debugger: pdb.

python

```python
import pdb
pdb.set_trace()
```

3. **Interactive Debugging with IDEs**:

- o Use debugging tools in IDEs like PyCharm or VSCode to set breakpoints and step through code.

2.2. Debugging Common Pipeline Issues

1. **Data Mismatch**:
    - o Check schemas and data types using pandas:

    python

    ```
    print(df.dtypes)
    ```

2. **Missing Data**:
    - o Identify and handle missing values:

    python

    ```
    print(df.isnull().sum())
    ```

3. **Performance Bottlenecks**:
    - o Profile code execution with cProfile:

    bash

    ```
    python -m cProfile -o output.prof pipeline.py
    ```

    - o Visualize performance with snakeviz:

    bash

```
pip install snakeviz
snakeviz output.prof
```

4. Broken Dependencies:

- o Verify library versions:

bash

```
pip freeze
```

2.3. Debugging Distributed Pipelines

For distributed frameworks like Spark:

1. Enable Logging:

python

```
spark =
SparkSession.builder.appName("DebugPipeline").getOrCreate()
spark.sparkContext.setLogLevel("DEBUG")
```

2. Inspect Sample Data:

python

```
df.show(n=10, truncate=False)
```

3. Use Web UI:

- o Access Spark Web UI to monitor jobs: http://<driver-host>:4040.

---

3. Ensuring Pipeline Reliability with Automated Testing

3.1. Automating Tests

1. **Integrating Tests with CI/CD**:
   - o Use tools like GitHub Actions, Jenkins, or GitLab CI to automate testing.
   - o Example: GitHub Actions Workflow:

   ```yaml
   yaml

   name: CI

   on: [push]

   jobs:
     test:
       runs-on: ubuntu-latest
       steps:
       - uses: actions/checkout@v2
       - name: Set up Python
         uses: actions/setup-python@v2
         with:
           python-version: '3.9'
   ```

```
- name: Install dependencies
  run: pip install -r requirements.txt
- name: Run tests
  run: pytest
```

3.2. End-to-End Testing

Test entire pipelines by simulating real-world scenarios.

- **Example: Testing an ETL Pipeline**:

    python

    ```python
    from etl_pipeline import import run_pipeline

    def test_etl_pipeline():
        output = run_pipeline("test_input.csv", "test_output.csv")
        assert output["rows_processed"] > 0
    ```

3.3. Data Validation Frameworks

Use frameworks like **Great Expectations** for data quality checks.

- **Install and Initialize**:

    bash

    ```bash
    pip install great_expectations
    great_expectations init
    ```

- **Example Check**:

python

```
from great_expectations.dataset import PandasDataset

df = PandasDataset({"age": [25, 30, None]})
result = df.expect_column_values_to_not_be_null("age")
print(result.success)  # False
```

3.4. Load Testing

Test pipeline performance under load using tools like **Apache JMeter** or **Locust**.

- **Locust Example**:

python

```
from locust import HttpUser, task

class LoadTestUser(HttpUser):
    @task
    def test_api(self):
        self.client.get("/api/data")
```

Run with:

bash

```
locust -f load_test.py
```

4. Practical Example: Debugging and Testing an ETL Pipeline

1. **Pipeline Code**:

python

```python
import pandas as pd

def etl_pipeline(input_file, output_file):
    try:
        # Extract
        df = pd.read_csv(input_file)

        # Transform
        df = df.dropna().reset_index(drop=True)
        df['value'] = df['value'] * 2

        # Load
        df.to_csv(output_file, index=False)
        return {"rows_processed": len(df)}
    except Exception as e:
        print(f"Error: {e}")
        raise
```

2. **Test Code**:

python

```python
from etl_pipeline import etl_pipeline
```

```
def test_etl_pipeline():
    output = etl_pipeline("test_input.csv", "test_output.csv")
    assert output["rows_processed"] == 100
```

3. **Debugging an Error**:

   o Add print() statements or use a debugger to trace issues in the pipeline.

Testing and debugging are essential for building reliable data pipelines. Unit testing with pytest ensures individual components function as expected, while debugging tools help resolve runtime issues. Automated testing and validation frameworks further enhance pipeline reliability, making your workflows robust and scalable. In the next chapter, we'll explore advanced analytics and machine learning integration in data engineering workflows.

Chapter 21: Performance Optimization

Optimizing the performance of your data pipelines is crucial for scalability, efficiency, and ensuring timely processing of large datasets. This chapter will cover techniques for profiling Python code using cProfile and line_profiler, applying parallel and concurrent programming with multiprocessing and asyncio, and optimizing memory usage for large datasets.

1. Profiling Python Code with cProfile and line_profiler

1.1. What is Code Profiling?

Profiling helps you identify performance bottlenecks in your code by measuring how much time is spent on each function or line. This allows you to target specific areas of the code for optimization.

1.2. Profiling with cProfile

cProfile is a built-in Python module for profiling the performance of your code.

- **Basic Usage**:

python

```python
import cProfile

def slow_function():
    total = 0
    for i in range(1000000):
        total += i
    return total


cProfile.run('slow_function()')
```

This will output statistics such as function calls, execution time, and number of calls for each function.

- **Output**:

lua

```
1000001 function calls in 0.123 seconds
  ncalls  tottime  percall  cumtime  percall filename:lineno(function)
       1    0.000    0.000    0.123    0.123  <ipython-input-1-
d1d1badd4b7b>:1(slow_function)
       1    0.000    0.000    0.000    0.000 {built-in method builtins.exec}
       1    0.000    0.000    0.000    0.000 <string>:1(<module>)
     ...
```

- **Sorting by Time**: To sort the output by cumulative time, use:

bash

```
python -m cProfile -s cumtime your_script.py
```

1.3. Profiling with line_profiler

line_profiler provides more granular profiling, showing time spent on individual lines of code.

- **Installation**:

    bash

    pip install line_profiler

- **Usage**:

    1. Add the @profile decorator to the function you want to profile:

        python

        ```
        @profile
        def slow_function():
            total = 0
            for i in range(1000000):
                total += i
            return total
        ```

    2. Run the profiler:

        bash

kernprof -l -v your_script.py

- **Output**:

sql

Timer unit: 1e-06 s

Total time: 0.123456 s
File: your_script.py
Function: slow_function at line 4

Line #	Hits	Time	Per Hit	% Time	Line Contents
4					@profile
5	1	0.000	0.000	0.0	total = 0
6	1000001	123456	0.000	100.0	for i in range(1000000):
7	1	0.000	0.000	0.0	return total

2. Parallel and Concurrent Programming with multiprocessing and asyncio

2.1. What is Parallelism and Concurrency?

- **Parallelism**: Running tasks simultaneously on multiple processors or cores.

- **Concurrency**: Managing multiple tasks at once, where tasks may run in parallel or sequentially depending on system resources.

2.2. Using multiprocessing for Parallelism

The multiprocessing module allows you to leverage multiple CPU cores to run tasks in parallel.

- **Basic Example**: Parallelizing a task across multiple processes.

python

```
import multiprocessing

def square(n):
    return n ** 2

if __name__ == '__main__':
    with multiprocessing.Pool() as pool:
        result = pool.map(square, [1, 2, 3, 4, 5])
        print(result)  # Output: [1, 4, 9, 16, 25]
```

- **Explanation**:
  - Pool.map() distributes tasks across available processors.

- This parallelization improves performance for CPU-bound tasks.

2.3. Using asyncio for Concurrency

asyncio is useful for managing I/O-bound tasks, like web scraping or reading from disk, without blocking other operations.

- **Basic Example**:

python

```python
import asyncio

async def fetch_data():
    await asyncio.sleep(1)
    return "data"

async def main():
    data = await fetch_data()
    print(data)

asyncio.run(main())
```

- **Explanation**:
  - asyncio.sleep(1) simulates an I/O operation (e.g., downloading data).

    o The event loop allows other tasks to run during waiting times.

2.4. Combining multiprocessing and asyncio

For mixed workloads (I/O-bound and CPU-bound), combining multiprocessing and asyncio can improve performance.

- **Example**: Run CPU-bound tasks in parallel while managing I/O-bound tasks concurrently.

python

```python
import asyncio
import multiprocessing

def cpu_task(n):
    return n ** 2

async def io_task(n):
    await asyncio.sleep(1)
    return f"Data {n}"

async def main():
    with multiprocessing.Pool() as pool:
        cpu_results = pool.map(cpu_task, [1, 2, 3, 4, 5])
        io_results = await asyncio.gather(*[io_task(i) for i in range(5)])
        print(cpu_results)
        print(io_results)
```

```
asyncio.run(main())
```

3. Optimizing Memory Usage for Large Datasets

3.1. Memory Management in Python

Efficient memory usage is crucial when working with large datasets.

- **Reducing Memory Footprint**:
  - Use generator expressions instead of lists for large datasets.
  - Example:

    python

    ```python
    # List comprehension (memory-heavy)
    numbers = [i * 2 for i in range(1000000)]

    # Generator expression (memory-efficient)
    numbers_gen = (i * 2 for i in range(1000000))
    ```

- **Use numpy for Numerical Data**: numpy arrays are more memory-efficient than lists for numerical data.

  python

  ```python
  import numpy as np
  ```

```
data = np.array([1, 2, 3, 4, 5])
print(data.nbytes)  # Memory usage in bytes
```

3.2. Using pandas with Large Datasets

pandas can consume a lot of memory when working with large datasets. Here are a few ways to optimize memory usage:

1. **Use dtype to Reduce Memory Usage**: Specify column data types when loading data to reduce memory footprint.

   python

   ```
   import pandas as pd

   dtype = {'col1': 'int32', 'col2': 'float32'}
   df = pd.read_csv('large_data.csv', dtype=dtype)
   ```

2. **Load Data in Chunks**: For large CSV files, load data in smaller chunks.

   python

   ```
   chunk_size = 100000
   chunks = pd.read_csv('large_data.csv', chunksize=chunk_size)
   for chunk in chunks
       process(chunk)  # Process each chunk
   ```

3. **Dropping Unnecessary Columns**: Drop unused columns to save memory.

python

```python
df = df.drop(columns=['unnecessary_column'])
```

3.3. Optimizing with Dask

For large datasets that don't fit in memory, **Dask** provides parallelized operations on chunks of data, similar to pandas.

- **Example**:

  python

  ```python
  import dask.dataframe as dd

  # Load a large CSV file
  ddf = dd.read_csv('large_data.csv')
  result = ddf.groupby('column').sum().compute()   # Compute result in parallel
  ```

4. Practical Example: Optimizing a Data Pipeline

1. **Initial Pipeline (Inefficient)**:

   python

```python
import pandas as pd

def process_data(file_path):
    df = pd.read_csv(file_path)
    df['new_col'] = df['old_col'] * 2
    return df

data = process_data('large_data.csv')
```

2. **Optimized Pipeline**:

python

```python
import pandas as pd

def process_data(file_path):
    dtype = {'old_col': 'float32'}
    df = pd.read_csv(file_path, dtype=dtype, usecols=['old_col'])
    df['new_col'] = df['old_col'] * 2
    return df

data = process_data('large_data.csv')
```

3. **Parallelized Pipeline with Dask**:

python

```python
import dask.dataframe as dd

def process_data(file_path):
    ddf = dd.read_csv(file_path, dtype={'old_col': 'float32'})
```

```
ddf['new_col'] = ddf['old_col'] * 2
return ddf.compute()


data = process_data('large_data.csv')
```

Optimizing performance in data pipelines involves profiling code to identify bottlenecks, leveraging parallel and concurrent programming for better resource utilization, and optimizing memory usage for large datasets. By utilizing tools like cProfile, multiprocessing, asyncio, and Dask, you can build more efficient and scalable data pipelines. In the next chapter, we will explore advanced data integration techniques.

Chapter 22: Machine Learning in Data Engineering

Data engineers play a critical role in the machine learning (ML) workflow by preparing and managing data, creating pipelines, and ensuring that ML models can be deployed and maintained at scale. This chapter will explore the role of data engineers in ML workflows, discuss techniques for preprocessing data for ML models, and cover the creation of pipelines to deploy these models effectively.

1. Role of Data Engineers in ML Workflows

1.1. Data Engineering in the ML Pipeline

Data engineers are responsible for ensuring that data is available, clean, and structured for machine learning models to train and make predictions. They work closely with data scientists to build and maintain the infrastructure that supports ML workflows.

- **Key Responsibilities**:
    - o **Data Collection and Ingestion**: Gather and store data from various sources (databases, APIs, logs, etc.).

- o **Data Transformation**: Clean, aggregate, and reshape data for use in ML models.

- o **Data Storage**: Organize and manage large datasets efficiently using databases, data lakes, or cloud storage.

- o **Pipeline Orchestration**: Create automated workflows that move data between systems, ensuring it is consistently and efficiently prepared for ML models.

1.2. ML Workflow Overview

1. **Data Collection**: Data engineers gather raw data from various sources.

2. **Data Preprocessing**: Cleaning, transforming, and enriching the data for ML use.

3. **Feature Engineering**: Extracting meaningful features from raw data.

4. **Model Training**: Data scientists build and train ML models using the prepared data.

5. **Model Evaluation and Testing**: Ensuring the model's performance is acceptable.

6. **Model Deployment**: Data engineers work on creating scalable pipelines to deploy models into production.

7. **Model Monitoring and Maintenance**: Continuously monitor model performance and manage updates.

1.3. Tools and Technologies in ML Engineering

- **Data Processing**: Apache Spark, Dask, Pandas.
- **Data Storage**: AWS S3, Google Cloud Storage, HDFS, SQL/NoSQL databases.
- **ML Frameworks**: TensorFlow, PyTorch, Scikit-learn.
- **Pipeline Orchestration**: Apache Airflow, Kubeflow, Prefect.

2. Preprocessing Data for ML Models

2.1. Importance of Data Preprocessing

Data preprocessing is essential for ML models to perform well. Raw data is often noisy, incomplete, or inconsistent. Data preprocessing includes various techniques that clean, structure, and transform raw data into a format that ML models can learn from effectively.

2.2. Common Data Preprocessing Steps

1. **Handling Missing Values**:

   o **Imputation**: Replace missing values with a mean, median, or mode.

   o **Drop**: Remove rows or columns with missing values.

python

```
import pandas as pd

df = pd.read_csv('data.csv')

# Impute missing values with the mean
df.fillna(df.mean(), inplace=True)

# Drop rows with missing values
df.dropna(inplace=True)
```

2. **Scaling and Normalization**:

   o Normalize numerical features so they are on a similar scale, improving the model's efficiency.

python

```
from sklearn.preprocessing import StandardScaler

scaler = StandardScaler()
df_scaled = scaler.fit_transform(df[['feature1', 'feature2']])
```

3. **Encoding Categorical Data**:

o Convert categorical variables into numerical form using one-hot encoding or label encoding.

python

```
# One-hot encoding
df = pd.get_dummies(df, columns=['category_column'])

# Label encoding
from sklearn.preprocessing import LabelEncoder
encoder = LabelEncoder()
df['encoded_column'] = encoder.fit_transform(df['category_column'])
```

4. **Feature Engineering**:
   o Create new features from existing data to improve model performance.

python

```
df['new_feature'] = df['feature1'] * df['feature2']
```

5. **Data Transformation**:
   o Apply techniques such as logarithmic transformations to handle skewed data distributions.

python

```
import numpy as np
df['log_transformed'] = np.log(df['feature'])
```

6. **Handling Outliers**:

   o Detect and manage outliers to prevent them from distorting the model.

   python

   ```
   # Remove rows where 'feature' is beyond 3 standard deviations from the mean
   df = df[(df['feature'] - df['feature'].mean()).abs() < 3 * df['feature'].std()]
   ```

2.3. Data Splitting

Split data into training and testing datasets to evaluate model performance.

- **Example**:

  python

  ```
  from sklearn.model_selection import train_test_split

  X = df.drop('target', axis=1)
  y = df['target']

  X_train, X_test, y_train, y_test = train_test_split(X, y, test_size=0.2, random_state=42)
  ```

3. Building Pipelines for ML Model Deployment

3.1. Importance of ML Pipelines

Once the model is trained, it needs to be deployed in a production environment. This involves creating a pipeline that automates the data ingestion, preprocessing, model prediction, and output handling. A reliable pipeline ensures consistency and scalability when serving ML models.

3.2. Creating an End-to-End ML Pipeline

1. **Data Ingestion**: Ingest real-time or batch data into the pipeline.
   - o Use APIs, databases, or file systems to feed data into the pipeline.
   - o Example:

   python

   ```
   import requests

   def fetch_data():
       response = requests.get('https://api.example.com/data')
       return response.json()
   ```

2. **Preprocessing**: Apply the preprocessing techniques described earlier (e.g., scaling, encoding, etc.).

   o Integrate this into the pipeline as a series of steps.

   o Example using Scikit-learn pipeline:

   python

   ```python
   from sklearn.pipeline import Pipeline
   from sklearn.preprocessing import StandardScaler
   from sklearn.ensemble import RandomForestClassifier

   pipeline = Pipeline([
       ('scaler', StandardScaler()),
       ('classifier', RandomForestClassifier())
   ])
   pipeline.fit(X_train, y_train)
   ```

3. **Model Prediction**: Use the trained model to make predictions on new data.

   o Example:

   python

   ```python
   predictions = pipeline.predict(X_test)
   ```

4. **Model Deployment**: Deploy the pipeline using Flask, FastAPI, or a cloud service (e.g., AWS Lambda, GCP Cloud Functions).

   o Example using Flask to expose the model via an API:

python

```
from flask import Flask, request, jsonify

app = Flask(__name__)

@app.route('/predict', methods=['POST'])
def predict():
    data = request.get_json()
    # Preprocess the data and predict
    prediction = pipeline.predict([data['input']])
    return jsonify({'prediction': prediction.tolist()})

if __name__ == '__main__':
    app.run(debug=True)
```

5. **Continuous Monitoring**: Once the model is deployed, continuously monitor its performance to ensure that it remains accurate over time.

   o   Implement logging and alerting for anomalies in the model's performance.

3.3. Automating and Orchestrating Pipelines

Use tools like **Apache Airflow, Kubeflow**, or **MLflow** to automate and orchestrate machine learning workflows.

- **Example: Automating with Apache Airflow**:

1. Install Apache Airflow:

bash

```
pip install apache-airflow
```

2. Define a DAG (Directed Acyclic Graph) for an ML workflow:

python

```
from airflow import DAG
from airflow.operators.python_operator import PythonOperator
from datetime import datetime

def train_model():
    # Your ML training code here
    pass

dag = DAG('ml_pipeline', start_date=datetime(2023, 1, 1))

train_model_task = PythonOperator(task_id='train_model', python_callable=train_model, dag=dag)

train_model_task
```

3.4. Model Versioning and Rollback

Ensure that you can version and rollback models as needed.

- **Using MLflow**:

bash

pip install mlflow

Track models and their performance metrics:

python

import mlflow

```
mlflow.start_run()
mlflow.log_param("param_name", param_value)
mlflow.log_metric("metric_name", metric_value)
mlflow.sklearn.log_model(model, "model")
mlflow.end_run()
```

---

4. Practical Example: Building an ML Pipeline

Scenario: Create an end-to-end pipeline for training and deploying an ML model that predicts housing prices.

1. **Data Ingestion**: Fetch housing data from a URL.
2. **Data Preprocessing**: Clean and preprocess the data (handle missing values, encode categorical features).
3. **Model Training**: Train a regression model on the data.
4. **Deployment**: Deploy the model using Flask as a web service for predictions.

Data engineers play a pivotal role in ensuring that machine learning models are effectively integrated into production workflows. By preprocessing data, building automated pipelines, and deploying models, data engineers create scalable, reliable ML systems. In the next chapter, we'll explore best practices for managing and monitoring data pipelines at scale.

Chapter 23: Real-Time Analytics

In the age of big data, the ability to process and analyze data in real-time has become increasingly important. Real-time analytics allows businesses to make immediate data-driven decisions, improve customer experiences, and optimize operations. This chapter introduces real-time analytics, explains how to build dashboards using Flask and Dash, and discusses integrating real-time data pipelines with business intelligence (BI) tools.

1. Introduction to Real-Time Analytics

1.1. What is Real-Time Analytics?

Real-time analytics refers to the process of continuously analyzing and extracting insights from data as it is generated. Unlike batch processing, where data is processed at scheduled intervals, real-time analytics enables instant decision-making based on current data.

- **Key Benefits**:
  - **Instant Insights**: Analyze data as it arrives for immediate action.

- o **Enhanced Decision Making**: Make real-time adjustments to business processes, such as inventory management or pricing.
- o **Improved Customer Experience**: Personalize customer interactions based on live data.

1.2. Use Cases for Real-Time Analytics

- **Financial Services**: Detect fraud in financial transactions in real time.
- **E-commerce**: Provide personalized recommendations based on user behavior.
- **IoT**: Monitor and respond to sensor data from devices in real time.
- **Customer Support**: Track customer sentiment in real time to improve service quality.

1.3. Real-Time Data Sources

- **Streamed Data**: Data generated continuously from sources like sensors, websites, and applications.
- **Message Queues**: Platforms like Apache Kafka, RabbitMQ, and AWS Kinesis manage real-time data streams.
- **APIs**: Real-time data can be ingested via API calls, such as social media feeds or financial market data.

2. Building Dashboards with Flask and Dash

2.1. Introduction to Dash

Dash is a Python framework for building web-based data dashboards that display real-time data in an interactive way. It is built on top of Flask, Plotly, and React.js, making it simple to create interactive and visually appealing dashboards.

- **Key Features**:
  - **Interactivity**: Users can interact with charts and data tables.
  - **Ease of Use**: Dash is user-friendly and requires minimal front-end knowledge.
  - **Real-Time Data**: Dash can be integrated with real-time data streams to create live dashboards.

2.2. Installing Dash

Install Dash and its dependencies:

bash

```
pip install dash
pip install plotly
```

2.3. Building a Simple Real-Time Dashboard with Dash

- **Example: Real-Time Stock Price Dashboard**: Here, we'll create a simple dashboard to visualize stock prices in real time.

    1. **Create the app.py File**:

        python

        ```python
        import dash
        from dash import dcc, html
        import plotly.graph_objs as go
        import random
        import time

        app = dash.Dash(__name__)

        # Layout of the dashboard
        app.layout = html.Div([
            html.H1('Real-Time Stock Price Dashboard'),
            dcc.Graph(id='live-graph', animate=True),
            dcc.Interval(
                id='graph-update',
                interval=1*1000,  # Update every second
                n_intervals=0
            )
        ])
        ```

```python
# Callback function to update the graph
@app.callback(
    dash.dependencies.Output('live-graph', 'figure'),
    [dash dependencies.Input('graph-update', 'n_intervals')]
)
def update_graph(n):
    # Simulate stock price data
    x_data = list(range(n))
    y_data = [random.uniform(100, 500) for _ in x_data]

    figure = {
        'data': [go.Scatter(
            x=x_data,
            y=y_data,
            name='Stock Price',
            mode='lines+markers'
        )],
        'layout': go.Layout(
            title='Stock Price Over Time',
            xaxis={'title': 'Time'},
            yaxis={'title': 'Price (USD)'}
        )
    }
    return figure

if __name__ == '__main__':
    app.run_server(debug=True)
```

2. **Run the Application**:

bash

python app.py

3. **Access the Dashboard**: Open a browser and go to http://127.0.0.1:8050/ to see the real-time stock price updates.

2.4. Adding More Complex Interactivity

Dash supports multiple types of components such as sliders, dropdowns, and text inputs to allow users to customize the data they view.

- **Example: Adding a Dropdown for Stock Selection**:

python

```python
app.layout = html.Div([
    html.H1('Real-Time Stock Price Dashboard'),
    dcc.Dropdown(
        id='stock-dropdown',
        options=[
            {'label': 'Stock A', 'value': 'A'},
            {'label': 'Stock B', 'value': 'B'}
        ],
        value='A'
    ),
```

```python
    dcc.Graph(id='live-graph', animate=True),
    dcc.Interval(
        id='graph-update',
        interval=1*1000,
        n_intervals=0
    )
])


@app.callback(
    dash.dependencies.Output('live-graph', 'figure'),
    [dash.dependencies.Input('graph-update', 'n_intervals'),
     dash.dependencies.Input('stock-dropdown', 'value')]
)
def update_graph(n, stock):
    # Generate stock data based on selection
    y_data = [random.uniform(100, 500) for _ in range(n)]
    figure = {
        'data':            [go.Scatter(x=list(range(n)),            y=y_data,
mode='lines+markers')],
        'layout': go.Layout(
            title=f'{stock} Stock Price Over Time',
            xaxis={'title': 'Time'},
            yaxis={'title': 'Price (USD)'}
        )
    }
    return figure
```

3. Integrating Real-Time Pipelines with BI Tools

3.1. What are Business Intelligence (BI) Tools?

BI tools are software applications used to analyze, visualize, and report on data. Popular BI tools include Power BI, Tableau, and Looker. These tools provide real-time insights by connecting to data pipelines and processing live data.

3.2. Connecting Real-Time Data Pipelines to BI Tools

1. **Real-Time Data Ingestion**:
   - Use **Kafka**, **RabbitMQ**, or **AWS Kinesis** to stream data into BI tools.
2. **Example: Real-Time Analytics with Tableau**:
   - **Direct Connection**: Connect your data warehouse or database (e.g., Google BigQuery, AWS Redshift) to Tableau for live querying and visualization.
   - **Streaming Data**: Use Tableau's built-in support for live data connections to directly ingest real-time data.
3. **Automating Data Refreshes**:
   - Use **Apache Airflow** or **AWS Lambda** to automatically trigger data updates from real-time streams to your BI tools.

3.3. Building a Data Pipeline for BI Integration

1. **Set up a Kafka Stream**:
   - Use **Apache Kafka** for real-time data streaming.
2. **Stream Data to a Database**:
   - Use **Kafka Connect** to stream data to a database like PostgreSQL or AWS Redshift.
3. **Connect BI Tool to the Database**:
   - Use the BI tool's native connectors to pull real-time data from the database and display it on dashboards.

3.4. Use Case: Real-Time Marketing Dashboard

A real-time marketing dashboard can integrate data from multiple sources like social media feeds, website traffic, and sales metrics. The dashboard can track live campaign performance, showing metrics such as impressions, clicks, and conversions.

- **Pipeline**:
  1. Collect data from APIs (social media, website analytics).
  2. Use Kafka or AWS Kinesis to stream this data.
  3. Store data in a cloud database (e.g., Redshift or BigQuery).
  4. Display live data on a Dash or Tableau dashboard.

4.

Real-time analytics empowers organizations to make fast, data-driven decisions by processing and visualizing data as it is generated. Dashboards built with tools like Flask and Dash provide interactive, live visualizations of data, while BI tools offer advanced analytics capabilities. By integrating real-time data pipelines into your workflow, you can enhance business operations, customer experiences, and decision-making. In the next chapter, we will explore how to scale data pipelines for big data environments.

Chapter 24: Case Studies in Data Engineering

Real-world case studies are invaluable for understanding how data engineering principles are applied across different industries. This chapter explores end-to-end implementations of data engineering pipelines across e-commerce, finance, and healthcare, highlighting lessons learned and best practices that can be applied to various data engineering workflows.

1. End-to-End Implementation of Data Engineering Pipelines

1.1. Overview of Data Engineering Pipelines

A typical data engineering pipeline involves several stages: data ingestion, data cleaning and transformation, storage, analytics, and sometimes real-time data processing. The goal is to create a seamless flow of data that can be processed, analyzed, and made accessible for business stakeholders.

An end-to-end pipeline includes:

1. **Data Ingestion**: Collecting data from various sources like databases, APIs, or real-time streams.

2. **Data Transformation**: Cleaning, filtering, and shaping the data to make it useful for analysis.

3. **Data Storage**: Storing the data in structured or unstructured formats (e.g., data lakes, data warehouses).

4. **Data Analytics/Modeling**: Running analytics or machine learning models on the data.

5. **Data Visualization/Reporting**: Delivering insights via dashboards or reports.

1.2. Key Components of an End-to-End Data Pipeline

- **Data Sources**: APIs, databases, files, or real-time streams.

- **Ingestion Framework**: Tools like Apache Kafka, AWS Kinesis, or Apache Nifi for collecting data.

- **Data Processing**: Tools like Apache Spark, Apache Flink, or Pandas for data cleaning, transformation, and analytics.

- **Storage Solutions**: Cloud storage services (S3, GCS), data warehouses (Redshift, Snowflake), or NoSQL databases (DynamoDB, MongoDB).

- **Orchestration**: Workflow orchestration using Apache Airflow or managed services like AWS Step Functions or Google Cloud Composer.

- **Reporting/Visualization**: BI tools (Tableau, Power BI) or custom dashboards built using frameworks like Dash or Flask.

---

2. Case Studies from E-Commerce, Finance, and Healthcare

2.1. E-Commerce: Customer Behavior Analysis

Problem: An e-commerce company wanted to analyze customer behavior to personalize product recommendations, optimize pricing strategies, and predict future sales.

Solution:

1. **Data Ingestion**:
   - Collected customer behavior data (clicks, views, purchases) from website logs and APIs.
   - Data streamed in real-time using Kafka.
2. **Data Processing**:
   - **Batch Processing**: Used Apache Spark for aggregating large volumes of historical customer interaction data.
   - **Real-Time Processing**: Implemented real-time processing using Apache Flink to process data

streams and provide real-time insights for personalized recommendations.

3. **Data Storage**:
   - o Data was stored in a **Data Lake** (Amazon S3) for raw data and **Redshift** for processed data to make it accessible for reporting.

4. **Data Analytics**:
   - o Applied machine learning models using **Scikit-learn** for customer segmentation and sales prediction.

5. **Reporting**:
   - o Dashboards were built with **Tableau** to track metrics like conversion rates, average order value, and customer lifetime value (CLV).

Lessons Learned:

- **Data Latency**: Managing real-time and batch data processing effectively was challenging, but using a hybrid approach (Apache Kafka for streaming and Spark for batch) helped balance the two.
- **Data Quality**: Ensuring clean and consistent data was critical, especially when dealing with real-time data streams.

2.2. Finance: Fraud Detection System

Problem: A financial institution needed a fraud detection system to analyze transactions in real time and flag suspicious activity.

Solution:

1. **Data Ingestion**:
   - Data was ingested from financial transaction systems via Kafka in real time.
   - Historical transaction data was stored in a **SQL database** (PostgreSQL) for deeper analysis.

2. **Data Processing**:
   - **Real-Time Processing**: Used **Apache Spark Streaming** to process transaction data in real time.
   - The system used machine learning models to detect patterns of fraudulent behavior (e.g., unusual spending or login activity).

3. **Data Storage**:
   - Transaction data was stored in a **data warehouse** (Amazon Redshift) for analytics and reporting.

4. **Analytics and Model Building**:
   - Built predictive models using **Logistic Regression** and **Random Forests** in Scikit-learn to identify anomalies in transaction patterns.

5. **Reporting**:

- o **Power BI** dashboards were used to provide insights into the number of fraudulent transactions and associated risk factors.

Lessons Learned:

- **Model Performance**: Continuous monitoring and retraining of the fraud detection model were necessary to account for evolving fraud tactics.
- **Scalability**: Ensuring the system could scale during peak transaction times, such as holidays or promotions, required careful resource management and optimization.

2.3. Healthcare: Patient Data Analytics

Problem: A healthcare provider wanted to analyze patient data to improve treatment outcomes, reduce hospital readmission rates, and optimize resource allocation.

Solution:

1. **Data Ingestion**:
   - o Data from electronic health records (EHR) was ingested through APIs and batch processes.
   - o Patient data was stored in a **NoSQL database** (MongoDB) for flexible schema management.
2. **Data Processing**:

- o **Batch Processing**: Used **Apache Spark** for aggregating and transforming patient data from multiple sources (EHR, lab results, medical imaging).
- o **Real-Time Processing**: Used **Apache Kafka** to stream real-time patient data such as vital signs and alerts from monitoring devices.

3. **Data Storage**:
   - o Combined data was stored in a **data lake** (AWS S3) and also aggregated in a **data warehouse** (Google BigQuery) for reporting and analysis.

4. **Analytics**:
   - o Applied machine learning models to predict patient risk factors, using **TensorFlow** for deep learning models on patient records and lab results.

5. **Reporting and Visualization**:
   - o Created **custom dashboards** in **Dash** for healthcare professionals to view real-time patient statuses and predictive analytics regarding treatment and risk.

Lessons Learned:

- **Data Privacy**: Ensuring compliance with **HIPAA** was critical, and encryption was applied at all stages of the data pipeline.

- **Data Quality**: The quality of medical data was often inconsistent, requiring extensive cleaning and validation before it could be used for modeling.

3. Lessons Learned and Best Practices

3.1. Data Quality and Integrity

- **Best Practice**: Consistently validate, clean, and preprocess data to ensure high-quality input for models and analytics.
- **Lesson Learned**: Data pipelines must include robust checks to handle missing, corrupted, or inconsistent data, especially when dealing with multiple data sources.

3.2. Scalability and Performance

- **Best Practice**: Design pipelines to be scalable and resilient to handle large data volumes, especially during peak times.
- **Lesson Learned**: Implementing parallel processing and distributed computing frameworks (e.g., Apache Spark, Kafka) ensures pipelines can handle big data effectively.

3.3. Real-Time Data Processing

- **Best Practice**: Use hybrid architectures for real-time and batch processing, integrating stream processing tools (Kafka, Flink) with batch processing tools (Spark).
- **Lesson Learned**: Real-time data processing requires careful consideration of latency, throughput, and system performance. Buffering data and ensuring efficient message handling is critical.

3.4. Model Monitoring and Retraining

- **Best Practice**: Continuously monitor machine learning models and set up automated retraining pipelines to adapt to changing patterns in the data.
- **Lesson Learned**: Machine learning models can degrade over time due to changes in data patterns, so it's important to monitor and retrain models regularly.

4.

Data engineering plays a critical role in enabling data-driven decision-making across industries like e-commerce, finance, and healthcare. The case studies presented here demonstrate the importance of building scalable, resilient, and efficient data pipelines to handle large volumes of data, integrate real-time data, and make insights accessible for end-users. By following best practices and continuously optimizing pipelines, data engineers can help organizations unlock the value of their data. In the next chapter, we will discuss the future of data engineering and emerging technologies in the field.

Chapter 25: Advanced Tools and Libraries

As data engineering tasks grow in complexity and scale, it becomes essential to use advanced tools and libraries to manage workflows, distribute processing, and scale systems effectively. This chapter introduces advanced tools like Dask, Prefect, and Luigi, compares them for workflow management and scaling, and discusses how to leverage community resources for learning and collaboration.

1. Overview of Advanced Libraries

1.1. Dask

Dask is a flexible and powerful parallel computing library in Python designed for handling larger-than-memory datasets. It extends common Python tools like **pandas**, **NumPy**, and **scikit-learn** to work in parallel on distributed systems.

- **Key Features**:
    - o **Parallel Processing**: Dask allows parallel execution of tasks across multiple CPUs or distributed clusters.

- o **Scalability**: It scales from a single machine to large clusters, enabling data processing on datasets that don't fit into memory.
- o **Integration with Pandas and NumPy**: Dask DataFrames and Arrays offer an intuitive interface similar to pandas and NumPy but for distributed computing.
- o **Task Scheduling**: Dask includes its own task scheduler for efficient parallel execution.
- **Example**: Processing large datasets with Dask:

python

```python
import dask.dataframe as dd

# Read large CSV file
ddf = dd.read_csv('large_file.csv')

# Perform computation on the data
result = ddf.groupby('column_name').mean().compute()
```

- **When to Use Dask**:
  - o Working with large datasets that exceed memory limits.
  - o Parallel processing with minimal setup.

1.2. Prefect

Prefect is a modern workflow management system designed for automating, scheduling, and monitoring data workflows. It focuses on providing a user-friendly interface for building and orchestrating pipelines, with built-in features for failure recovery, retries, and logging.

- **Key Features**:
  - **Flexible Workflow Orchestration**: Prefect allows the creation of complex workflows using tasks and dependencies.
  - **Easy-to-Use UI**: Prefect offers a simple UI for monitoring, managing, and visualizing workflows.
  - **Failover and Recovery**: Built-in features for handling task retries, failure detection, and recovery.
  - **Cloud Integration**: Prefect integrates easily with cloud environments like AWS, Google Cloud, and Azure.
- **Example**: A simple Prefect flow:

python

```
from prefect import task, Flow

@task
def hello_world():
    print("Hello, world!")
```

```
with Flow("hello-flow") as flow:
   hello_world()

flow.run()
```

- **When to Use Prefect**:
    - Orchestrating complex workflows.
    - Handling failure recovery and retries.
    - Managing workflows in the cloud.

1.3. Luigi

Luigi is another Python package for building complex pipelines of batch jobs. It is widely used in environments where tasks depend on each other, and where jobs are frequently retried.

- **Key Features**:
    - **Task Dependency Management**: Luigi helps define and manage task dependencies, ensuring tasks are executed in the correct order.
    - **Scheduler**: It provides a task scheduler for managing the execution of large workflows.
    - **Visualization**: Luigi includes a web interface for visualizing pipeline dependencies and job statuses.
- **Example**: Defining tasks with Luigi:

python

```
import luigi

class TaskA(luigi.Task):
    def run(self):
        with self.output().open('w') as f:
            f.write('Hello, world!')

class TaskB(luigi.Task):
    def requires(self):
        return TaskA()

    def run(self):
        with self.input().open('r') as f:
            print(f.read())

if __name__ == '__main__':
    luigi.run()
```

- **When to Use Luigi**:
    - Handling batch jobs and complex task dependencies.
    - When workflows require retries and logging.

---

2. Comparing Tools for Workflow Management and Scaling

2.1. Dask vs. Prefect vs. Luigi

Feature	Dask	Prefect	Luigi
Workflow Orchestration	Limited (focused on parallelism)	Strong, with built-in retry logic	Strong, with dependency management
Ease of Use	Simple for those familiar with pandas and NumPy	User-friendly UI and integrations	Command-line interface, less UI focus
Scalability	Excellent (scalable across clusters)	Cloud-ready with easy scaling	Works well on single machines
Task Scheduling	Built-in scheduling for parallel tasks	Advanced task scheduling and retry logic	Built-in task scheduler
Best for	Large-scale data processing	Orchestrating complex workflows	Managing batch jobs and dependencies
Integration with Cloud	Works with cloud-based resources	Strong cloud integrations (AWS, GCP)	Can be integrated with cloud tools

2.2. Choosing the Right Tool

- **Use Dask** when you need to scale data processing from a single machine to a cluster while maintaining compatibility with Python data libraries like pandas and NumPy.
- **Use Prefect** when building complex workflows that require robust task orchestration, retry policies, and cloud integration.
- **Use Luigi** for managing and orchestrating batch jobs with complex dependencies, especially if you need a task scheduler and visualization tools.

---

3. *Leveraging Community Resources for Learning and Collaboration*

3.1. Online Communities and Forums

- **Stack Overflow**: A go-to resource for resolving coding issues and learning from community discussions on best practices.
- **GitHub**: Explore open-source repositories, contribute to projects, or access documentation for libraries like Dask, Prefect, and Luigi.

- **Reddit**: Subreddits such as /r/dataengineering and /r/MachineLearning are excellent places for discussions and questions on data engineering tools.

3.2. Documentation and Tutorials

- **Dask Documentation**: Comprehensive guides on using Dask for parallel computing and data processing (Dask Docs).
- **Prefect Documentation**: Learn about Prefect workflows, task orchestration, and cloud deployment (Prefect Docs).
- **Luigi Documentation**: A detailed guide for setting up and using Luigi for batch job management (Luigi Docs).

3.3. Webinars, Meetups, and Conferences

- **Data Engineering Meetups**: Many cities host data engineering-specific meetups where professionals share knowledge on tools and techniques.
- **Conferences**: Events like Strata Data Conference, Data EngConf, and PyData provide a great way to stay up-to-date on industry trends and learn about new tools.

3.4. Open Source Projects and Contributions

- Contributing to open-source projects is a great way to enhance your knowledge and collaborate with experts. Many of the tools mentioned (Dask, Prefect, and Luigi) are open-source and welcome contributions.
- **GitHub**: Contributing to repositories such as Dask GitHub, Prefect GitHub, and Luigi GitHub can provide hands-on experience with real-world projects.

4.

Advanced tools like Dask, Prefect, and Luigi are essential for building scalable, efficient, and reliable data engineering pipelines. By understanding their strengths and applications, you can choose the best tool for your use case. Leveraging community resources like documentation, forums, and conferences can accelerate your learning and provide opportunities for collaboration. Whether you're processing large datasets, orchestrating complex workflows, or managing batch jobs, these tools can help you optimize and automate your data engineering pipelines. In the next chapter, we'll explore the future trends in data engineering and the evolving landscape of big data technologies.

Chapter 26: The Future of Data Engineering

As the field of data engineering evolves, new technologies, trends, and methodologies continue to reshape how data is collected, processed, and analyzed. This chapter explores emerging trends in data engineering, the growing role of Python in big data and artificial intelligence (AI), and how data engineers can prepare for continuous learning and career growth.

1. Emerging Trends in Data Engineering

1.1. Data Engineering in the Cloud

Cloud platforms (AWS, Google Cloud, Azure) have become the backbone of modern data engineering workflows. These platforms provide scalable, flexible, and cost-efficient solutions for storing, processing, and analyzing data.

- **Serverless Computing**: Serverless architecture, such as AWS Lambda, allows for scalable compute power without managing infrastructure. This trend is growing in popularity as it reduces overhead and enables easier scaling.

- **Managed Services**: Tools like AWS Glue, Google BigQuery, and Azure Synapse Analytics provide fully managed services for data pipelines, reducing the complexity of deployment and maintenance.
- **Data Lakes and Data Warehouses**: The hybrid model of data lakes (e.g., AWS S3, Azure Data Lake) and data warehouses (e.g., Snowflake, Redshift) is allowing organizations to store both structured and unstructured data, making it easier to handle diverse data types.

1.2. Real-Time Data Processing

As businesses increasingly rely on real-time data, data engineering is moving towards real-time processing to deliver insights instantly.

- **Stream Processing**: Technologies like Apache Kafka, Apache Flink, and AWS Kinesis are enabling data engineers to handle real-time streams of data for immediate analysis and decision-making.
- **Event-Driven Architectures**: With real-time data, event-driven architectures allow systems to react to events as they occur, which is particularly useful in industries like finance, e-commerce, and healthcare.

1.3. Data Democratization and Self-Service Analytics

The trend toward **data democratization** means making data and analytics accessible to non-technical users.

- **Self-Service BI Tools**: Tools like Tableau, Power BI, and Looker empower business users to create dashboards and analyze data without relying on data engineering teams.
- **Data Governance**: As more people gain access to data, the need for strong data governance frameworks has grown. Data engineers will continue to be responsible for ensuring data security, quality, and compliance.

1.4. Machine Learning and AI Integration

Data engineering is becoming more closely integrated with machine learning and AI workflows. Data engineers are increasingly expected to work alongside data scientists to create seamless pipelines for ML model training, deployment, and monitoring.

- **ML Operations (MLOps)**: MLOps brings DevOps principles to machine learning, enabling continuous integration, continuous deployment, and monitoring of ML models.
- **Automated Data Preparation**: Automated feature engineering and data cleaning pipelines are essential to streamline the workflow from raw data to model-ready datasets.

1.5. Edge Computing

Edge computing refers to processing data closer to where it is generated (e.g., IoT devices), rather than sending all data to a centralized cloud server.

- **Use Cases**: Industries like manufacturing, transportation, and healthcare are adopting edge computing to reduce latency and enable real-time decision-making at the edge.
- **Tools and Frameworks**: Data engineers will need to work with distributed systems like Apache Kafka and Apache Flink to process data across multiple edge devices.

2. The Growing Role of Python in Big Data and AI

2.1. Python as the Language of Choice

Python has long been the preferred language for data engineering, thanks to its ease of use, rich ecosystem, and community support. Its popularity is only growing, especially in the realms of big data and AI.

- **Big Data**: Python integrates well with big data processing frameworks like Apache Spark and Dask, allowing data engineers to work with large datasets effectively.

- **AI and Machine Learning**: Python is the go-to language for building AI models, with libraries like **TensorFlow**, **Keras**, **PyTorch**, and **scikit-learn**. Data engineers are often involved in preparing data for AI models, managing data pipelines, and ensuring that AI systems operate efficiently in production environments.

2.2. Python Libraries for Big Data

- **Dask**: Dask extends pandas and NumPy for parallel computing on large datasets, making it easier to scale operations across a cluster.

- **PySpark**: PySpark provides a Python interface to Apache Spark, enabling data engineers to process large datasets in parallel across distributed systems.

- **Vaex**: Vaex is a high-performance library for working with large datasets that do not fit into memory, designed specifically for efficient and fast data exploration and manipulation.

2.3. Python in AI and MLOps

- **Data Pipeline Integration**: Python plays a key role in building the data pipelines that feed AI models. Libraries like **Airflow**, **Luigi**, and **Prefect** help manage workflows for training, testing, and deploying machine learning models.
- **MLOps Tools**: Tools like **MLflow**, **Kubeflow**, and **TensorFlow Extended (TFX)** are often used in combination with Python to implement automated workflows and integrate machine learning models into production systems.

2.4. Python for Automation and Cloud Integration

- **Cloud Services**: Python is widely used for automating cloud services and integrating with cloud providers like AWS, Google Cloud, and Azure. With libraries like **boto3** (AWS SDK), **google-cloud** (Google Cloud SDK), and **azure-sdk** (Azure SDK), data engineers can automate cloud-based tasks, such as provisioning resources, managing storage, and processing data.
- **Serverless Architectures**: Python is increasingly used in serverless computing platforms like **AWS Lambda**, allowing for scalable, event-driven applications.

3. Preparing for Continuous Learning and Career Growth

3.1. The Importance of Continuous Learning

Data engineering is a rapidly evolving field, and it's important for professionals to stay up-to-date with new tools, technologies, and best practices. Continuous learning will help data engineers remain competitive and adapt to the demands of their industry.

- **Adapting to New Tools**: Tools like **Dask**, **Prefect**, and **Apache Flink** are reshaping how data is processed and managed. Learning these tools will provide a competitive edge.
- **Embracing Automation and AI**: The rise of automation, AI, and machine learning in data pipelines means that data engineers must be comfortable working with these technologies to build and maintain intelligent systems.

3.2. Key Skills for the Future

- **Cloud Technologies**: Data engineers should be proficient in working with cloud platforms like AWS, GCP, and Azure. Cloud-native tools and serverless architectures are becoming standard in modern data engineering.

- **Big Data Tools**: Proficiency in big data frameworks such as Apache Spark, Hadoop, and Dask is essential for handling large datasets.

- **Machine Learning**: Understanding the basics of machine learning and how to prepare data for training and inference will be a significant advantage, especially as MLOps becomes more prevalent in data workflows.

- **Automation and Orchestration**: Experience with tools like Apache Airflow, Prefect, and Kubernetes for orchestrating complex workflows will be essential for managing scalable data pipelines.

3.3. Career Growth Paths

- **Data Engineer**: Focuses on building and maintaining data pipelines, ensuring data quality, and optimizing data processing workflows.

- **Data Architect**: Specializes in designing the architecture of data systems, ensuring scalability, and managing large-scale data infrastructure.

- **Machine Learning Engineer**: Works alongside data scientists to deploy and scale machine learning models, and ensures seamless integration with data pipelines.

- **Cloud Data Engineer**: Specializes in building and managing data pipelines in cloud environments, focusing on serverless architectures and cloud-based storage solutions.

3.4. Networking and Community Engagement

- **Conferences and Meetups**: Attending conferences like Strata Data Conference, PyData, and Data Engineering Summit is an excellent way to learn from industry leaders and network with peers.
- **Open-Source Contributions**: Contributing to open-source projects like Apache Airflow, Dask, or Prefect will improve your skills and connect you with the broader data engineering community.
- **Online Communities**: Join forums like Stack Overflow, Reddit's /r/dataengineering, and Data Engineering Slack channels to ask questions, share knowledge, and keep learning.

4.

The future of data engineering is full of exciting opportunities, driven by advances in cloud computing, big data, real-time processing, and machine learning. As a data engineer, staying ahead of emerging trends, mastering Python and its associated libraries, and focusing on continuous learning will ensure success in this dynamic field. By embracing new tools and technologies, data engineers can drive innovation and play a crucial role in the data-driven future of organizations.

www.ingramcontent.com/pod-product-compl.ance
Lightning Source LLC
La Vergne TN
LVHW022338060326
832902LV00022B/4112